All About Poetry 5

The East Of England

Edited by
Jonathan Fisher

This book belongs to

First published in Great Britain in 2010 by

Remus House
Coltsfoot Drive
Peterborough
PE2 9JX
Telephone: 01733 890066
Website: www.youngwriters.co.uk

All Rights Reserved
Book Design by Spencer Hart
© Copyright Contributors 2010
SB ISBN 978-0-85739-161-2

Foreword

At Young Writers our defining aim is to promote an enjoyment of reading and writing amongst children and young adults. By giving aspiring poets the opportunity to see their work in print, their love of the written word as well as confidence in their own abilities has the chance to blossom.

Our latest competition *Poetry Express* was designed to introduce primary school children to the wonders of creative expression. They were given free reign to write on any theme and in any style, thus encouraging them to use and explore a variety of different poetic forms.

We are proud to present the resulting collection of regional anthologies which are an excellent showcase of young writing talent. With such a diverse range of entries received, the selection process was difficult yet very rewarding.

From comical rhymes to poignant verses, there is plenty to entertain and inspire within these pages. We hope you agree that this collection bursting with imagination is one to treasure.

Contents

Hartley Primary School, Hartley
Ella Davies (9) 1
Megan Kelly (9) 2
Jack Hilditch (9) 3
Annabelle Holton (9) 4
James Silk (9) 5
Megan Townsend (9) 6
Chloë Milton-Robinson (9) 6
Sophie Francis (9) 7
Hannah Case (9) 7
Harry Downey (8) 8
Tyler Mabruki (9) 8
Teagan Higgins (8) 9
Ellis Smith (9) 9
Maddie Carruthers (9) 10
Zoe Jackett (8) 10
Cheyenne Dunn (9) 10
Matthew Adams (8) 11
Harry Hopgood (9) 11
Sammy Root (9) 11
Hannah Walker (9) 12
Ben Sutton (8) 12
Laura Robinson (9) 12
Juliet Clewes (8) 13
Liam Gregory (9) 13
Olivia Frost (9) 13
Billy Chambers (8) 13
Victoria O'Donoghue (9) 14

Kenninghall Community Primary School, Kenninghall
Ellie-Jean Royden (9) 14
Lottie Thurgar (7) 15
Hannah Shea (9) 15
Imogen Ungless (8) 16
Constance Peel (9) 16
Carys Fowler (9) 17
Felicity Hall (9) 17
Isobel Windle (8) 18
Hannah Panks (9) 18
Laura Lathan (8) 19
Elise Jefferis (8) 19

Georgina Chard (9) 20
Angus Clark (8) 20
Arthur Johnson (8) 21
Chelsea Duncan (9) 21
Aaron Powell (9) 22
Amy Duncan (7) 22
Chloe Yaxley (8) 22
George Collings (8) 23

Kingswood Junior School, Basildon
Sam Lee (8) 23
Tiffany Moorton (8) 23
Grace Stangar (7) 24
Amy Hayward (8) 24
Logan Croucher (9) 25
Jack Clarke (10) 26
Shannon Hernaman (11) 27
Molly Potter (8) 27
Adam Clarke (11) 28
Riley Chapman (9) 28
Robyn Pijuan-Winner (11) 29
Joe Ward-Threadwell (9) 29
Eden Akam (10) 30
Abylashaa Arulmoli (10) 30
Carmenella Hudson (11) 31
Suzi-Jo Stripe (11) 31
Mollie Anne Lloyd (11) 32
Libby Cox (11) 32
Josh Clarke (8) 33
Daniel Brazier (9) 33
Emily Clarke (11) 34
Illistyl Scates-stenzel (10) 34
Rebecca Allman (11) 35
Alex Corpuz (9) 35
Isobel McKeeve (10) 36
Gemma Rouse (10) 36
Emine Keskin (8) 37
Jeswin Babu (10) 37
Joe Eccles (8) 38
Bradley Gadsden (9) 38
Paris Casey (10) 39

Amy Coombs (9) ... 39
Ross Pigrum (10) ... 40
Nikhil Gokani (11) ... 40
Sophia McCarthy (9) ... 41
Jessica Daugirda (10) ... 41
Georgia Bell (10) ... 42
Ciaran Butler (8) ... 42
Alex Nathan Porter (9) ... 43
Sam Jones (10) ... 43
Grace O'leary (9) ... 44
Kai Dockerill (10) ... 44
Cally Blake (8) ... 45
Callum Bowring (10) ... 45
Savani Kale (8) ... 46
Josh Grayer (9) ... 46
Jodie Bland (8) ... 47
Faith Everett (9) ... 47
Zoe Allman (7) ... 48
Jack Potter (10) ... 48
Kuhle Nobanya (8) ... 49
Olivia Bond (11) ... 49
Oliver Stewart (10) ... 50
Hannah Morris (8) ... 50
Jack Evans (8) ... 51
Lauren Knell (9) ... 51
Haydn Bamfield (9) ... 52
Ben Campbell (8) ... 52
Harrison Essam (8) ... 53
Olivia Fitzpatrick (7) ... 53
Natasha Rael (8) ... 54
Isabel Buncher (8) ... 54
Jasmine North (9) ... 55
Nathan Cano-Lopez (8) ... 55
Holly Ann Morrish (8) ... 56
Brooke Macvicar (8) ... 56
Riley Shaw (8) ... 57
Chloe Macvicar (8) ... 57
Millie Dawson (7) ... 58
Lewis Bunce (8) ... 58
Coel Sharp (9) ... 59
Maddie MacLeod (8) ... 59
Adesola Faniyi (8) ... 60
Sam Francis (8) ... 60
Alfie Fisher (8) ... 61
Nishita Gadi (10) ... 61
Ella Maginn (9) ... 62
Daniel Lambart (8) ... 62
Willow Legg (7) ... 63
Emma Murton (7) ... 63
Theo Stedman-Redican (8) ... 64
Daisy Brunt (8) ... 64

Little Thurrock Primary School, Grays
Charlie Wright (9) ... 65
Bradley Jones (11) ... 66
Esme Lucking (9) ... 67
Tommy Mason (11) ... 68
Isabella Martin (10) ... 69
Daniel Tagg (8) ... 69
Leoni Pring (10) ... 70
Caitlan Matthews (9) ... 70
Alicia Bridge (9) ... 71
Hannah Phillips (9) ... 71
Hannah Obie (9) ... 72
Olivia Burns (10) ... 72
Molly Johnson (9) ... 73
Scott Regan (11) ... 73

Luton Junior School, Chatham
Nitin Chatrath (8) ... 74
Stephanie Southgate (7),
Rayjay Haswell, Harry Neill,
Jake Carroll, Jake Mockford (8),
Brunthavan Ratnasingham (9)
& Lucas Harvat (11) ... 74
Stephanie Southgate (7) ... 75
Charlotte Lewis (8) ... 75
John Sawyer (8) ... 75
Jessica Buckley (8) ... 76
Tommy Barfoot (8) ... 76
Keziah Dakat (8) ... 77
Jake Carroll (8) ... 77
Emily Ager (8) ... 78
Ellie James (8) ... 78
Ellie Cooper (7) ... 78
Brandon Richards (8) ... 79
Alex Newman (7) ... 79
Brooke Sandwell (8) ... 79
Bradley Harris (7) ... 80
Olivia Cox (8) ... 80
Molly Fray (8) ... 80
Charlotte O'Gallagher (8) ... 81
Amy Geoghegan (8) ... 81
Joseph Petty (8) ... 81

Moreton Hall Preparatory School, Bury St Edmunds
Tim Gilbey (11) 82
Issy Rush (11) 83

Oakfields Montessori School, Upminster
Oliver Heazel (11) 84
Adam Williams (11) 85
Beth Wilson (11) 86
Ellie Healy (9) 87
Morgan Miles (8) 88
Bethany Bradley (11) 89
Ben Kinder (11) 90
Layla Choudhury (9) 90
Sophie Gilkes-Tarsey (8) 91
Zain Ansari (9) 91
Henry O'Leary (9) 92
Patrick Mulroy-Yourell (9) 92
Raman Aval (11) 93
Emily Gilkes-Tarsey (11) 93
Michael Wenman (11) 94
Mia Choudhury (10) 94
Rachel Harvey (8) 95

Oaklands School, Loughton
Emily Edinburgh (9) 95
Elizabeth Davis (9) 96
Isabella Singer (9) 96
Holly Hembury (8) 97

St Joseph's RC Primary School, Barking
Kayla Stone (9) 97
Chantel-Marie Atayi (10) 98
Elson Simoni (10) 98
Eimear Browne (10) 99
Cristina Mascia (10) 99
Laurynas Neverauskas (10) 99
Paula Matovu (9) 100
Arthur Anyanjo (10) 100
Dylan Nirde (10) 101
Emily Peace (10) 101
Jaden Toussaint (10) 102
Kofi Agyeman Boamah (8) 102
Darragh Wilson (10) 103
Nathan Vitorino (10) 103
Linpaul Rodney (10) 104

Clayton Bokanga (9) 104
Rochelle McLaren (9) 105
Conor Jason (10) 105
Danielle Parker (9) 106
Oshi-Ada Idagu (10) 106
Carl King (8) 107
Chloe Okerago (8) 107
Ethan Dixon (8) 108
Elyas Ribeiro Cretu (7) 108
Dischan Mofaya Kimpini (7) 109
Sharanya Kilbert (8) 109
Callum Jason (8) 110
Mateusz Swiecicki (8) 110
Jade Flannery (8) 111
Harry Webster (8) 111
Suganya Kinslirobad (8) 112
James Hunt (8) 112

Skippers Hill Manor School, Mayfield
Elliott Glynn (8) 112
Isabelle Peach (10) 113
Amelia Field (10) 114
Sarah Shepherd (8) 114
Eliza Dunhill (10) 115
Francesca Plaskett (7) 116
Gabby Leach (9) 116
Louisa Hurel (10) 117
Jessy Leach (9) 117
Oscar Steward (9) 118
Ben Leach (10) 118
Lizzie Webb (9) 119
Matthew Scates (9) 119
Thomas Stone (10) 120

The Heritage School, Cambridge
Jacob Robson (9) 120
William Buchanan (7) 121
Robert Carter (8) 121
Alex Keller (7) 122
Jennifer Bell (8) 122
Olivia Alderson (7) 123
Oliver Chapman (8) 123
Seth Fletcher (8) 124
Kane Blake (7) 124
Joanna Haylett (8) 125
Zachary Dampier-Kell (7) 125

Rosa Tate (7) 126
Bradley McMahon (7) 126
Catherine Smartt (7) 126

The Howbridge Infant School, Witham

Michael Maxted (7) 127
Funmilola Bamigbele (6) 127
Thomas Miranda (7) 128
Abbie Brown (7) 128
Ben Nixon (7) 129
Robyn Babbs (7) 129
Emma Walsh (7) 130
Teddy Creasey (7) 130
Ben Mawhood (6) 131
Fahima Uddin (7) 131
Baillie Mason (6) 132
Billy Simmons (7) 132
Elva Webb (7) 133
Rio King (7) 133
Sophie Jarvis (7) 134
Jack Nice (6) 134
Christopher Weeks (7) 135
Jacob Scott (6) 135
Abby Brooks (6) 136
Grace Austin-Hunt (7) 136
Kye Bedford-Ingram (7) 136
Lara Anderson (6) 137
Alicia Champion (7) 137

The Poems

Willow Class

A is for Annabelle and Alex who always smile.
B is for Ben who buckles his shoes.
C is for Charlotte, Chloe, Cheyenne and Conor who do that too.
D is for Daisy who likes horses, also Declan who's mates with the boy.
E is for Ella who likes playing with dogs and toys,
F is for friends that are in the class.
G is for Guy who likes pies.
H is for Harry Hop and Harry Gagg who like dogs.
I is for Izzy who likes playing with logs.
J is for Jessica, James and Jack who like the colour purple.
K is for Kiaran who laughs all the time.
L is for Lucy, Lily also Louise who are all friends.
M is for Miss Stereck our teacher and also Megan.
N is for nice people in our class.
O is for October, a month of the year.
P is for Phoebe who likes unicorns.
Q is for quiz which we do in class.
R is for rats that are not nice.
S is for Sammy who likes football.
T is for Teagan, Trinity and Tyler who like Bluewater.
U is for USA that is America.
V is for Victoria who likes red shoes.
W is for world that we are in.
X is for X-ray which some of us have had.
Y is for yoghurt that some of us like.
Z is for Zoe who likes to lick lollies.

I hope you enjoyed it.

Ella Davies (9)
Hartley Primary School, Hartley

ABC Animal Poem

A is for animals, which this poem is about,
B is for butterflies fluttering with a doubt.
C is for cat, I have one of them,
D is for dog, I've got one and a hen.
E is for elephants with their curly tails,
F is for fish with their shiny scales.
G is for gruffalos with their pointy spikes,
H is for horses, they love going on hikes.
I is for iguanas drinking some tea,
J is for jellyfish in the sea.
K is for kangaroo who jumps just like me,
L is for lions eating the meat with glee.
M is for monkeys, they are just like me,
N is for newts, they are funky.
O is for ostriches, you see them on telly,
P is for pigs, they are so smelly.
Q is for quails, they want to be high,
R is for robins, they can fly.
S is for snakes, they hiss,
T is for tigers, they kiss.
U is for unicorns, they fly,
V is for vultures, they fight.
W is for water hogs, they love water,
X is for xylota, a small insect of course.
Y is for Yeval, the horse,
Z is for zebra eating its main course.

Megan Kelly (9)
Hartley Primary School, Hartley

Food, Just Food

A is for apple that is so juicy.
B is for banana that likes riding bikes.
C is for choccy chocolate that is really tasty.
D is for dragon fruit.
E is for silly billy eggs.
F is for fruity fruit.
G is for grapey grapefruit.
H is for smelly belly haddock.
I is for icy ice cream.
J is for slippery, slippery jelly.
K is for kiwi.
L is for sour, sour lemon.
M is for yellow melon.
N is for nectarine.
O is for bling, bling orange.
P is for yummy dummy passion fruit.
Q is for Quavers.
R is for smelly radish.
S is for big fat sausages.
T is for tacos.
U is for Utterly Butterly.
V is for vegetables.
W is for cheesy Wotsits.
X is for Xmas food.
Y is for yummy food.
Z is for zebra legs.

Jack Hilditch (9)
Hartley Primary School, Hartley

Year 4 Poem

A is for Alex who does funny accents.
B is for Ben who plays rugby.
C is for Chloe and Charlotte who laugh a lot.
D is for Declan who plays football.
E is for Ella who's obsessed with dogs.
F is for French we do with Mr Crosby.
G is for Guy who's fabulous at art.
H is for Harry H and Harry G who love go-karting.
I is for ink pens (the ink goes everywhere).
J is for Jasmine and Jessica who love crisps.
K is for Kieran who supports Arsenal.
L is for Lucy who likes lemonade.
M is for me who is crazy.
N is for numeracy which is fun maths.
O is for Olivia who's crazy about ponies.
P is for Phoebe who has a cute guinea pig.
Q is for quiet reading (which on our own is fun).
R is for Ryan who is very funny.
S is for Sammy who scores super goals.
T is for Teagan, Trinity and Tyler who like Bluewater.
U is for uniforms that we have to wear.
V is for Vicky who loves shoes.
W is for my class, Willow!
X is for xylophones that we use in music.
Y is for 'Yes Miss Sterecka' our class teacher.
Z is for *zzzzzzz* at the end of the day.

Annabelle Holton (9)
Hartley Primary School, Hartley

Alphabet Poem

A is for Anne, who drives a white van.
B is for Barry, who is as happy as Larry.
C is for Clare, who has lots of hair.
D is for Dennis, who likes playing tennis.
E is for Ellie, who likes watching telly.
F is for Frank, who once robbed the bank.
G is for Guy, who is very shy.
H is for Holly, who likes sucking a lolly.
I is for Izzy, who is very busy.
J is for Josh, who is very posh.
K is for Ken, who lives at the den.
L is for Lilly, who is very silly.
M is for Mike, who likes riding a bike.
N is for Neil, who once had a meal.
O is for Olly, who likes pushing a trolley.
P is for Pete, who has smelly feet.
Q is for the Queen, who likes being seen.
R is for Roger, who's named after Dodger.
S is for Sam, whose favourite food is ham.
T is for Trace, who can't keep up the pace.
U is for Unger, who has lots of slumber.
V is for Vic, who's best friends with Mick.
W is for Willy, who is very silly.
X is for Xavi, who is very savvy.
Y is for Yvette, who does not have a pet.
Z is for Zena, who is such a meaner.

James Silk (9)
Hartley Primary School, Hartley

Alphabet Poem

A is for Annabelle who likes horses,
B is for Ben who likes his pen,
C is for Charlotte who likes guinea pigs,
D is for Daisy who is so lazy,
E is for Ella who likes to draw,
F is for Freddie who likes Eddie,
G is for George who likes dance,
H is for Harry who likes Larry,
I is for Isabella who likes Ella,
J is for Jessica who likes chocolate,
K is for Kieran who likes Arsenal,
L is for Lucy whose best friend is Lily,
M is for Megan who likes scary music,
N is for number one who likes to be alive,
O is for Olivia who likes to lie,
P is for Phoebe who likes to smile,
Q is for quiz, that makes you fizz,
R is for Rosie who likes her ponies,
S is for Spud who likes studs,
T is for Teagan who likes weaving,
U is for ulcer that you get in your mouth,
V is for Victoria who just joined our school,
W is for whiteboard that we have lots of,
Y is for yoghurt that is healthy,
Z is for zebras that live in Africa.

Megan Townsend (9)
Hartley Primary School, Hartley

Alfie The Budgie - Haiku

My budgie is green,
Likes long, summer, swishy grass
His name is Alfie.

Chloë Milton-Robinson (9)
Hartley Primary School, Hartley

Tiptoe

Tiptoe,
Tiptoe,
Here comes a mouse,
Scampering out from his treetop house.

Tiptoe,
Tiptoe,
Here comes a cat,
Out come his claws and his teeth go snap.

Tiptoe,
Tiptoe,
Here comes a dog,
He misses the mouse but catches a frog.

Tiptoe,
Tiptoe,
Here comes a tiger,
She sees her dinner which will end up inside her.

Tiptoe,
Tiptoe,
All quiet now,
Just a mouse in the corner and a cat going miaow.

Sophie Francis (9)
Hartley Primary School, Hartley

My Dog Named Biscuit

My dog Biscuit is as clever as can be
Because she hides behind trees
She's like a soft cloud swifting across the sky.

She scampers like a mouse in the kitchen or house.
You can't tell her off with her face
And that's why I love my dog, Biscuit.

Hannah Case (9)
Hartley Primary School, Hartley

Penguin

Penguin, penguin, slide on belly, up and down the ice
Slide on the water
Oh doesn't it feel nice!
Waddle, waddle, slip and slide
If you want to catch fish make sure you hide!
Snowy and cold, very icy
Don't nip, it's not nicey
I like your orange beak
Open it, make fish go *eek!*
You're mostly coloured white
Look at the iceberg, look at the height
And one looks like a slide
Wow look at the speed, you hide
You zoom really quickly down
You've turned my frown upside down!

Harry Downey (8)
Hartley Primary School, Hartley

All About Friends

Friends are fun to play with, they have games to play.
Friends are kind to you and try not to hurt you.
Friends are helpful, so if you fall over, they will help you up.
Friends are generous, if you ask for a bit of something, they might give you a bit.
Friends are happy, so if you are sad they can make you happy.
Friends are people who make you laugh if someone has made you upset.
Friends are people who never make you upset.
Friends make you happy.

Tyler Mabruki (9)
Hartley Primary School, Hartley

My Teacher

Miss Sterecka is as busy as a bee,
And she is very bouncy.
She always greets you with a smile,
All the while she'll still smile.
Her jet-black hair and her fiery red highlights
Look like a fire dying down.
She is affectionate, loving and gentle
Words cannot describe her.
Her gloomy haunted house boots
Make her able to touch the sky.
Her clothes are divine, crimson, blue and flowers too
She is phenomenal, kind hearted, perfection, incredible.
And do you know who she is . . . ?
Miss Sterecka.

Teagan Higgins (8)
Hartley Primary School, Hartley

My Penguins

Slip, slide,
Up and down,

Make my frown,
Turn upside down,

Slipping and sliding,
Down the town,

Oh what a clown!

Ellis Smith (9)
Hartley Primary School, Hartley

My Animal Riddle

I am grass green with bright red eyes.
I live in the rainforest.
I like to jump from place to place.
I am wet and slimy.
I like to swim.
I have orange little padded feet.
What am I?
A: A red-eyed tree frog.

Maddie Carruthers (9)
Hartley Primary School, Hartley

Snakes Climb Everywhere

Snakes climb so well
Up the trees they lie so still
Looking like branches sticking out
Suddenly a tongue appears
Run mouse, run, the snake has seen you!
The snake's mouth opens really wide,
The mouse disappears,
Where has it gone?

Zoe Jackett (8)
Hartley Primary School, Hartley

The Last Cat Before Time

The last cat before time
Lived in the zoo
But also couldn't go to the loo.
The last cat before time
Never had a tutu
But never remembered his name!

Cheyenne Dunn (9)
Hartley Primary School, Hartley

My Snail

My snail is very fast
But it always comes last.
My snail can skateboard,
Its tricks are so cool.
My snail is very small,
It is smaller than a bouncy ball.
My snail is my snail
And it is very cool.

Matthew Adams (8)
Hartley Primary School, Hartley

Fat Cat

Fat cat
Skinny cat
Sitting on the bright mat.

Fat cat
Skinny cat
Falls off the bright mat.
Splat!

Harry Hopgood (9)
Hartley Primary School, Hartley

Bogey Trouble

Watch your bogies as they grow.
Watch your bogies as they overflow.
Watch your bogies as they fall in the snow.
Watch your bogies as they really glow.
Watch your bogies as they fall on your toe.
Watch your bogies as they fall very low.
Watch your bogies . . . oh no!

Sammy Root (9)
Hartley Primary School, Hartley

Dolphin Fun

Doli Dolphin under the sea
Swimming about here and there
Doli Dolphin everywhere catching fish
Swimming about with its tail wiggling about.
Doli Dolphin.

Hannah Walker (9)
Hartley Primary School, Hartley

Fish In A Ditch!

I have fish in a ditch!
I have fish on a pitch!
I have fish in a . . .
I have fish . . .
Everywhere!

Ben Sutton (8)
Hartley Primary School, Hartley

Funky Fish Poem

F unky Fish lives in a fish tank.
I call her Speedy.
S he loves to eat very quickly.
H er grandad is slow as a snail.
    She is Funky Fish.

Laura Robinson (9)
Hartley Primary School, Hartley

A Frog's Exercise

Hippity, hippity, hop
Jump!
Leap!
Splish, splash, splosh
Gone!

Juliet Clewes (8)
Hartley Primary School, Hartley

Skating Snail

Skating snail,
Skating on the sink,
Slips on some soap,
And lands in my drink!

Liam Gregory (9)
Hartley Primary School, Hartley

Amazing Animals

Horses gallop all day long,
Owls tu-whit-tu-whoo all night through,
Rabbits crunch on their carrots fresh from the ground,
And I wonder about these animals all year round.

Olivia Frost (9)
Hartley Primary School, Hartley

Eating My Lunch

Licking my lips, I'm finding my prey.
I find a zebra - he tries to run away.
Crunch! Crunch! Crunch!
I've finally got my lunch!

Billy Chambers (8)
Hartley Primary School, Hartley

Shoes - Haiku

I like high-heeled shoes.
Shoes are bright, shoes are shiny.
I like sporty shoes.

Victoria O'Donoghue (9)
Hartley Primary School, Hartley

Huskies

I love the way the huskies run
As they are having lots of fun.

The spiky icicles fall onto the snowy wet ground
As the cloud-grey huskies go round and round.

Mountains soar above my head
As the sky turns a sunset red.

A little puppy has lost its mum
So that puppy is rather glum.

Suddenly it's getting cold
Look, there's a penguin that's rather old.

All the huskies are back again,
Now it's time to build the den.

As they build, warmness comes
Oh what lovely, cloud-grey huskies, they're
cute as tasty buns.

Ellie-Jean Royden (9)
Kenninghall Community Primary School, Kenninghall

A Hot Beach

It smells like a hot summery day
with a suncream smell as well.

It feels like a hot sandpit
sitting in the golden sun.

It looks like a boiling hot summer day
which is the start of summer.

It reminds me of my holiday in Greece
and people wearing suncream that sinks into your skin.

It tastes like stony hot sand
which has just been touched.

The colour of the hot beach is golden yellow
and the sea is light blue.

Lottie Thurgar (7)
Kenninghall Community Primary School, Kenninghall

Summer

The emerald-green grass glints in the yellow sunlight.
The blazing sun has lots of dazzling colours.
The prickling heat spikes me on the back as I leisurely stroll across my garden.
It gets hotter and hotter like a radiator on full blast.
The light dances on top of the delightful flowers swaying gently in the breeze.
I like the way the ripples in the water get bigger and bigger until suddenly *pop!* They're gone.
The smell of the barbecue wafts up my nose as the wonderful smell fills the air.

Hannah Shea (9)
Kenninghall Community Primary School, Kenninghall

Winter Wonders

It looks like a beautiful, magical, wonderful and silvery collage of joy.

It reminds me of sparkly glitter, snow and Christmas.

The winter makes me feel lively, strange, freezing and shivery like a giant freezer.

When I walk into the house I smell hot chocolate, marshmallows and pine trees.

Oh the colours, the beautiful colours are silver, white and grey like the high Himalayas.

Imogen Ungless (8)
Kenninghall Community Primary School, Kenninghall

Winter Wonderland

It smells fresh and plain.
Tickly snow freezes my nostrils.
Crystal blue and shimmering silver sparkle
across the landscape.
It's as far as the eye can see.
Dreams always come true.

It feels cold but delightful.
Snowy mountains are rocky and as hard as metal.
It reminds me of love and luck and hope and joy and
peace and freedom.

Constance Peel (9)
Kenninghall Community Primary School, Kenninghall

Ice Cream

Ice cream is as cold as a lovely winter's day.
It can come in all sorts of wonderful colours and funny sizes.
It smells of delicious red strawberries.
Ice cream reminds me of frozen ice, like bitter cold snow that has just floated onto the ground.
It is a squishy piece of white brie cheese melting slowly in the hot yellow sun.
It can taste of all sorts of wondrous, lovely flavours, like a yummy, runny smoothie.

Carys Fowler (9)
Kenninghall Community Primary School, Kenninghall

Polar Bear

It reminds me of white, fluffy clouds gradually floating through the delightful blue sky.

It tastes like spicy Japanese chicken marinated in a hot sauce.

The colour of silvery, white marshmallows sitting in the dark cupboard like a polar bear's skin.

It smells like dirty, wet snow that has been sitting on
Captain Scott's tent for eight weeks in the freezing North Pole.

Felicity Hall (9)
Kenninghall Community Primary School, Kenninghall

The Beach

B eside the beach I eat my ice cream,
   salty sea water washing up on the smooth, golden sand.
E ach child has built a big sandcastle,
   looking like a knight's palace.
A dolphin dashes drastically across the sea
   looking like a big blue puddle.
C hildren play upon the bay as I watch from a dark grey cliff.
H appy families, enjoying a day on the beach.

Isobel Windle (8)
Kenninghall Community Primary School, Kenninghall

Polar Bears

It feels like a giant ball of wool all fluffy and furry.
It smells like the smell of the fresh water from the sea.
It tastes like fresh mouth-watering meat.
It is a white, creamy colour.
It reminds me of a fluffy white kitten all curled up in a ball.
It looks like a fluffy piece of mashed potato.

Hannah Panks (9)
Kenninghall Community Primary School, Kenninghall

Ice-Cold

I ce-cold drinks are like ice cubes
C old like blackcurrants
E veryone likes ice-cold drinks

C risp, cold liquid
O nly I like ice-cold drinks
L icking at ice-cold drinks
D rinking it makes me feel special.

Laura Lathan (8)
Kenninghall Community Primary School, Kenninghall

Beach

It looks like little bits of popcorn scattered all over the place.
It reminds me of a hot summer's day on the side of a swimming pool.
It is orange and yellow like the sun and a peach.
It tastes like salty sea that is blue and freezing.
It feels like little bits of pollen falling off a beautiful tree.
It smells like food, apples, ice cream and drinks.

Elise Jefferis (8)
Kenninghall Community Primary School, Kenninghall

Penguins

It smells like slimy, fresh, watery fish.
It feels like a slimy, silky, wet, cold sausage.
It tastes like fresh fish, a bit slimy.
Its colour is black and white with a little bit of yellow and orange.
It reminds me of a black and white polar bear.
It looks like a swimming polar bear with its fluffy white skin puffing out in the water.

Georgina Chard (9)
Kenninghall Community Primary School, Kenninghall

Desert

Hot and cold, as big as you like,
As red as fire,
As clear as jelly,
As golden yellow as the sun,
As sparkly as a diamond.
The sand swaying from side to side with the wind.

Angus Clark (8)
Kenninghall Community Primary School, Kenninghall

Fire

Fire, fire, tastes of bacon burning in the dazzling red sun.
Fire, fire, looks like wild daffodils swaying in the wind.
Fire, fire, smells like boiled eggs.
Fire, fire, feels like hot burning trees.
Fire, fire, reminds me of sitting in my sitting room with the fire burning.

Arthur Johnson (8)
Kenninghall Community Primary School, Kenninghall

A Polar Bear

It is soft and fluffy like a creamy cloud.
It reminds me of my hamster called Boots.
It smells like a polar bear catching fish.
It is as white as snow.
It has fluffy ears and a mighty body.
Meat and goodness.

Chelsea Duncan (9)
Kenninghall Community Primary School, Kenninghall

The Ice

The ice glistens like a diamond in the amazing sun.
It feels as smooth as a pillow.
As hard as a rock.
As cold as Antarctica.
It reminds me of ice cubes in a drink on a hot summer's day.

Aaron Powell (9)
Kenninghall Community Primary School, Kenninghall

Dolphin

It is as blue as the sky.
It smells of juicy, smelly plankton.
It looks like it is a blue moon.
It feels like some wet fish.

Amy Duncan (7)
Kenninghall Community Primary School, Kenninghall

Hot Chocolate

It looks like gooey brown mud.
It tastes creamy.
It feels slimy.
It reminds me of the times I spent with my family.

Chloe Yaxley (8)
Kenninghall Community Primary School, Kenninghall

A Monkey

It is as brown as a bar of chocolate.
It smells of rotting bananas.
It is as furry as sheep.
It feels as soft as my teddy.

George Collings (8)
Kenninghall Community Primary School, Kenninghall

Love

Love is like kissing your mum.
Love looks like a baby's smile.
Love tastes like chocolate.
Love smells like strawberries.
Love feels like cuddling my dad.
Love is the colour blue like the sky.

Sam Lee (8)
Kingswood Junior School

Love

Love is red like red apples.
Love is the sound of my mum talking.
Love looks like a wheelbarrow of hearts.
Love feels like my dad talking to me.
Love smells like my dog having a bath.
Love tastes like eating chocolate.

Tiffany Moorton (8)
Kingswood Junior School

Sadness

Sadness looks like a tear dropping down a baby's eye.
Sadness sounds like a heart breaking in half.
Sadness smells like the fresh breeze going away.
Sadness feels like the fresh water dropping on my head.
Sadness is the colour of blue.
Sadness tastes of water falling down my throat.

Grace Stangar (7)
Kingswood Junior School

Love

Love is red like a lovely rose.
Love feels like hugging my family.
Love smells like melting chocolate.
Love sounds like my mum talking to me.
Love tastes like juicy strawberries.
Love sounds like my sister singing to me.

Amy Hayward (8)
Kingswood Junior School

Anger

I feel like monsoons bursting out of the ocean in a heavy rainstorm, creating a major earthquake as the mountains rise to crush everything in sight, like a fizzing bottle overflowing on
the kitchen floor.
I can hear the sirens of the falling bombs bullying the town with their explosions and flame friends.
I feel like being put in pressure as the houses topple on me.
I feel the explosions pushing me away, away, away, further, further, further until I have disappeared out of sight into the mist and ash of the no-longer-standing city of darkness.
You do not know how overwhelming the anger is bursting out of me.
The guns are firing in all directions.
My mind has gone completely blank.
I can't feel, hear or see anything, as I fall into a river, my clothes no longer on fire.
I'm just sinking, I can't push my way up to the surface because of my heavy clothes and then *smack!*
I have hit the seabed, hopelessly lying there forever.
I'm not sure whether to do nothing or give it a second try
But I'm paralysed, unable to move, my sight fading, my eyes closed forever, my body crawling across the dark seabed.

Logan Croucher (9)
Kingswood Junior School, Basildon

An Angry Emotion

I see the red on my body,
waiting there to burst,
annoyed and frustrated.
Who should I explode at first?

The insulting words get through my ears,
ringing like a bell,
but it was far too much for me.
I charged and down they fell.

I feel my skin prickling hard,
the flames burning on my face.
I shot the flames on him like a gun,
and he left there in a disgrace.

The words go down my nostrils,
blocking my nose, like a shield,
and once again I charged at him,
then left for the peaceful field.

I taste the speech, I swallow it down,
and fired it back up,
ripped it into several pieces,
then spit it on his head, like a cup.

My emotions of anger I cannot stop.
If it could just go, let it rot.
I roar with rage at my enemy,
and what I wanted I got.

Jack Clarke (10)
Kingswood Junior School, Basildon

Love

Love is the colour of red because it's the colour of your beating heart pumping your blood.

Love is the smell of chocolate melted on the stove.

Love is the sound of gentle footsteps tapping against the calm waves of the ocean.

Love is the taste of chocolate cake.
The taste of soft Belgian chocolates.

Love looks like the church two people get married in.
It looks like newborn animals growing up side by side with their mother.

Love feels like your heart only beats for that special someone.
It feels like the feeling you get when you cuddle someone you love.

Love reminds me of the day I brought my beautiful dog home and played with her all night.

Shannon Hernaman (11)
Kingswood Junior School, Basildon

Happiness

Happiness is the yellow sunshine beaming down at me.

Happiness feels like smooth and soft petals on a lovely flower.

Happiness looks like happy bunnies bouncing through the long wavy grass.

Happiness smells like a chocolate fountain with lovely marshmallows.

Happiness tastes like warm chocolate chip muffins.

Happiness sounds like two tweeting birds singing a lovely song.

Happiness is the shape of a kite in the sky, flying way up high.

Molly Potter (8)
Kingswood Junior School, Basildon

Silence

Silence is black and all dark colours,
It has nothing to say about itself.

Silence smells like rotten fish,
It is dead and quiet, very quiet.

Silence sounds like a banging of a door,
It is someone trying to escape the room of silence.

Silence tastes like water,
It is plain and boring on its own.

Silence looks like a lion,
It is trying to roar but has a croaky throat.

Silence feels like a never-ending wall,
Its surface is so smooth and so flat.

Silence reminds me of a black hole,
It is big, black and very deep, just like silence.

Adam Clarke (11)
Kingswood Junior School, Basildon

Happy

I smell someone baking cake.
Someone is cooking a roast beef.
The silk sheets on my bed.

You see West Ham playing against Spurs
And West Ham are winning.
England is about to win the World Cup.

I taste that onion bahji.
I can taste some pepperoni pizza.

I feel my silk blanket.
I feel the breeze blowing on me.

Riley Chapman (9)
Kingswood Junior School, Basildon

Happiness

The colour of happiness is baby blue, as blue, as clear, as on a summer's day.
Happiness smells of the sea creeping up to crash on the sand, my body feels relaxed and calm.
Sounds of waves slowly smashing against the soft sand,
as you know it will be a good day, because children splash
and crash on the water and waves.
Taste of happiness is when chocolate is melting in the warmth
of your mouth, making you want to eat more as it swirls, twirls
and whirls in your body.
If I could see happiness it would be an aeroplane floating past
with a soft cloud puffing behind it.
Happiness would feel like the warmth of the sun on your cold skin.
When my dad cheers for Barcelona as they score,
that is the thing that reminds me of happiness.

Robyn Pijuan-Winner (11)
Kingswood Junior School, Basildon

Angry

I feel like
I am going to
burst like a volcano.
I hear people
speaking and
shouting in my head.
I feel a wall
of rock and stone.
I see blue
and red like
something is burning
into ash like a
bomb has just exploded.

Joe Ward-Threadwell (9)
Kingswood Junior School, Basildon

Frustrated With Anger

I feel like a volcano
bursting out with its ash
burning down to the floor,
spreading everywhere.
I touch the fuzziness
of the volcano.
Anger is bursting through me like fire
I smell the wildness of burning
from the trees and hot ash.
I taste the fire when I am breathing in.
I see the red, boiling explosion oozing
out of the hot volcano.
I hear banging of falling down trees
the splashing from the bubbling volcano.

Eden Akam (10)
Kingswood Junior School, Basildon

Happy Farm

I feel like a horse galloping in freedom,
over the mountains and under the sea.

I hear horses neighing and cows mooing for a rhythm,
blue birds tweeting, sheep baaing, all in a rhythm.

Smelling fresh air with a hint of rotting hay,
makes me taste corn and health.

Touching the animals and touching the flowers,
makes me want to sing and dance.

Feeling the soft petals with my own hands,
makes me feel special in my heart.

A farm is a nice place,
filled with animals and happiness.

Abylashaa Arulmoli (10)
Kingswood Junior School, Basildon

Love

Love is rich blood-red, like the colour of roses.

Love smells like a huge bar of chocolate unwrapped and ready to eat.

Love sounds like a newly born baby's heartbeat.

Love tastes of freshly cooked bacon, sausages and baked beans, yum . . .

Love looks like a dove flying in the blue sky, swooping and diving for joy.

Love feels like the fur of my dog once she's been groomed.

Love reminds me of the shimmering moon on a warm evening in summer.

Carmenella Hudson (11)
Kingswood Junior School, Basildon

Love

Love is the colour of a beautiful red rose newly blossomed.

Love is the sound of gentle waves folding over and over the golden sand.

Love smells of my favourite perfume - fresh and light.

Love tastes like melted chocolate as you sip it from your cup.

Love looks like a dozen red roses all huddled together swaying with the wind.

Love feels like the silkiness of your pyjama bottoms as you slide your legs into them.

Love reminds me of the day two people met and instantly knew that they were the one for them.

Suzi-Jo Stripe (11)
Kingswood Junior School, Basildon

Love

Love is red like my heart, it is the colour of roses which are presented to your true love.

Love is the smell of pasta and a barbecue cooking outside in the summer day.

Love is the sound of birds singing from the highest branch of a tree.

Love is the taste of cheese and onion crisps crumbling in my mouth.

Love is the look of my sister's kitten staring into my eyes.

Love is the feel of soft puppies in my arms.

Love reminds me of my family, it shows me how much I am cared for and needed.

Mollie Anne Lloyd (11)
Kingswood Junior School, Basildon

Happiness

Happiness is the colour of a field full of multicoloured flowers, gleaming in the sunlight.

Happiness smells of a delicious breakfast cooking as I wake up in the morning.

Happiness sounds like children laughing and birds chirping.

Happiness tastes like freshly baked cakes with delicious strawberry icing on top.

Happiness looks like the sun shining down onto lush green grass.

Happiness feels like velvet running through my fingers.

Happiness reminds me of laughing and playing with all my friends.

Libby Cox (11)
Kingswood Junior School, Basildon

Just Because Someone Made Fun Of Me . . .

I went as fast as a Bugatti Veyron,
As strong as Hulk,
As mad as an earthquake,
As big as Mount Everest!
Just because someone made fun of me . . .
I had a fiery tummy,
In my tummy I had anger bubbles,
I went as loud as an explosion,
As hard as rocks,
As unstoppable as Superman.
Just because someone made fun of me . . .

Josh Clarke (8)
Kingswood Junior School, Basildon

I Can Do Anything

I can do anything without a fright,
Rummaging through the jungle all night.
A mountain to climb,
A place to find.
I'm as brave as a lion,
I'll eat anything.
Worms, you should try them.
When I do any of these
I really do get pleased,
Happy, joyful, proud of myself.
I can do anything
I really can.

Daniel Brazier (9)
Kingswood Junior School, Basildon

Sadness

If sadness was a colour it would be grey because of the rainy days.
If sadness was a smell it would be burning fire stealing your
memories of the good times.
If sadness was a sound it would be the sobbing of a child crying.
If sadness was a taste it would be salty tears trickling down
your face.
If you could see sadness it would be an unhappy child sulking in
the corner of a room.
If you could feel sadness it would be the cold marble of a loved
one's headstone.
Sadness reminds me of poor children being starved because they
don't have any food.

Emily Clarke (11)
Kingswood Junior School, Basildon

Happy

I feel like a flower about to be kissed by my handsome prince.
When I am happy I see lovely flowers and hearts dancing
all around me.
I can also see my nine-month-old puppy waiting for me.
When I touch the hot pizza, it burns my hands.
When I taste the cheese, it melts in my mouth,
I feel like I'm in Paradise.
When I smell the home-made pizza I can taste it in my mouth.
As I hear people calling me over to play a game, I feel happy outside
and inside.
I can also hear ponies waiting for me to ride on them.
When I am happy I can do all of these things.

Illistyl Scates-stenzel (10)
Kingswood Junior School, Basildon

Fun!

Fun is the colour yellow, like the bright sun smiling down at me.
Fun smells like crispy chips, which I eat at lunchtime.
Fun sounds like music to my ears, which is played
by a wonderful orchestra.
Fun tastes like a freshly picked but ripe orange, while sitting
on top of a hill.
Fun feels like smooth seashells, presented neatly in the calm ocean.
Fun looks like a group of birds flying across the blue sky.
Fun reminds me of walking on the sandy beaches (late at night)
as the sand curls round my toes.
Nothing could be as good as fun!

Rebecca Allman (11)
Kingswood Junior School, Basildon

Upset

I can hear the clouds pouring water down my face.
The cold breeze wiping away my tears, like a handkerchief.
Tasting sadness in my throat and feeling my heart pounding slowly.
The taste of shame on my lips.
Walking around, with my head down.
Crying like I'm making a flood.
So sick of being lonely, so tired of tears.
I'm so sad and slow.
The sun setting down and the moon coming up.
What a sad day it was.

Alex Corpuz (9)
Kingswood Junior School, Basildon

Angry

I feel like a bomb about to explode,
My anger burning like volcanic ash.
The things I hear inside my head,
I can smell bad and horrid smells all around.
The anger I can taste in my mouth,
I can see explosive stuff in my mind
On what I should do when I'm angry.
Everything ringing around me which is very loud.
I get a bad temper when I am furious
As if my head is going to explode.

Isobel McKeeve (10)
Kingswood Junior School, Basildon

Revenge

Revenge is indigo, like the shining night sky.
It sounds like screaming children running through a stream.

Revenge tastes of dirt, like a mouldy old banana left out to die.
It smells like sour, evil lemons, ready to fight back!

Revenge feels like a shooting pain going through your heart.
It looks like an exploding water balloon ready to get you!

Revenge reminds me of hate, like my sister and I having
an argument!

Gemma Rouse (10)
Kingswood Junior School, Basildon

My Baby Brother

In the hospital when I saw you lying in your cot,
I was so happy you were mine.

You're so cute with dinky toes and little soft feet and hands,
Nails so short, and a little soft delicate head.

My dream was to have a baby brother
And that came true.

I love my brother so much
And this is all true.

Emine Keskin (8)
Kingswood Junior School, Basildon

Anger

I feel like a bomb going to explode,
like a volcano about to erupt.
I can taste burning anger in my mouth,
so hot I can't hold it in anymore.
I can taste bitterness in my mouth,
so bad tasting I feel like spitting it out.
I can hear chattering with anger.
My heart is thumping so fast I feel sick.
I can feel hot tears in my eyes.

Jeswin Babu (10)
Kingswood Junior School, Basildon

Anger

Anger is like bombs with ash and fire surrounding homes.
Anger smells like rotting sores.
Anger looks like lava and ash.
Anger tastes like rotting flesh.

Joe Eccles (8)
Kingswood Junior School, Basildon

My Nan

H aving ice cream on a very sunny day,
A lbums to listen to.
P laces to go to,
P laying at the park on a sunny day,
I like looking at my nan's cockatiels,
N an, you are the best nan in the world,
E xciting stuff awaits us,
S eeing movies and car racing,
S eeing sea lions and dolphins performing.

Bradley Gadsden (9)
Kingswood Junior School, Basildon

Happy

I can see flowers, pink beautiful flowers.
Birds, blue birds flying in the air.
I can touch pink petals from the flowers,
soft and silky.
I can smell the flowers mixed in with fine fresh air.
I can hear the birds singing a song for everyone
to listen to, while children are playing in the park.
I can taste the salad crunch in my mouth
that makes me go crazy.

Paris Casey (10)
Kingswood Junior School, Basildon

Summer

It's a hot sunny day when I'm sweating and baking.

When I'm going to a beach I get all wet
but watch out for the crabs because you might get caught.

I feel so much pain from the pinch of a crab.

Amy Coombs (9)
Kingswood Junior School, Basildon

Sadness

Sadness is the colour of grey
Like an old doll's house falling away.
It smells like a stuffed-up nose
And rain touching your toes.
Silent and joyless like an empty room.
The taste of sand and seawater
Reminds me of the beaches of Normandy.
Grey and dark like at a funeral,
Reminds me of black.

Ross Pigrum (10)
Kingswood Junior School, Basildon

Love

Love is velvet red like your blood as it pumps around your body.
Love smells of newly fallen rain as it hits the ground.
Love sounds like football fans singing songs for their team when they score a goal.
Love tastes like delicious Harrod's chocolate melting in my mouth.
Love looks like Man United winning the Premier League.
Love feels like a hot summer's day as the sun shines down on me.
Love reminds me of Manchester United beating Barcelona for the Champions League.

Nikhil Gokani (11)
Kingswood Junior School, Basildon

My Baby Sister

I love you so much, so don't go away,
S ometimes I want to squeeze you too much,
L ullabies calm you to go to sleep,
A re you there, there you are, awake again.

Sophia McCarthy (9)
Kingswood Junior School, Basildon

Surprise

Surprise is yellow, like the sun rising and warm summer mornings.
It bubbles violently like fireworks exploding inside of you.

Surprise sounds like balloons popping noisily at my birthday party.
It smells of deliciously baking chocolate cake, reaching out to me.

Surprise reminds me of a Christmas party, with the chatter of happy people being reunited with their friends.
It tastes like a delicious pouch of popping candy, pushing its way through my mouth.

Jessica Daugirda (10)
Kingswood Junior School, Basildon

I Feel Proud

I feel proud, I smell a beautiful smell.
I feel proud, my mind sees a happy place.
I feel proud, I taste a wonderful taste
Not strong, not weak but just, just right.
I feel proud, gently I touch things,
Bubbly things I feel.

Soft, smooth, calm sounds, quiet noises . . .

I think to myself, *I feel proud!*

Georgia Bell (10)
Kingswood Junior School, Basildon

Puppies

My puppy's little tongue licks your hand.
His eyes stare at mine.
His tail starts to wag.
When he licks me it feels funny.
His cute smile makes me happy.

Ciaran Butler (8)
Kingswood Junior School, Basildon

BMXing

Sunny day, good day to do BMXing today.
I am going to do stunts.

I am very sweaty from that race.

I won the race today,
It's the best day of my life.

I have butterflies because
I am on the start gate.

Alex Nathan Porter (9)
Kingswood Junior School, Basildon

Pain

Pain is as black as burning toast
and tastes like spicy chillies.
It sounds like a baby screaming in hunger.
It's like being punched for evermore,
like a bomb wreckage.
It reminds me of a nightmare!
Pain is as black as burning toast,
but not as good as Sunday roast!

Sam Jones (10)
Kingswood Junior School, Basildon

Hayden

H ugs me when I'm sad
A lways cheers me up
Y ou're the best baby cousin
D on't go away because I love you too much
E very day you cuddle me
N ever leave my sight.

Grace O'leary (9)
Kingswood Junior School, Basildon

Anger

A nger, I feel anger when I get called a name.
 I feel like a volcano about to erupt.
N asty, I feel nasty when I get shouted at. I feel like a bull running at a red sheet.
G uilty, I feel guilty when my friends have got something when I haven't.
E veryone is so nice they let me play all the time.
R age, I feel rage, I am a shark about to attack its prey.

Kai Dockerill (10)
Kingswood Junior School, Basildon

Love

Love is bright pink like roses.
Love tastes like food you'll always love.
Love feels like bright, pink love hearts.
Love smells of hot chillies.
Love sounds like lovely music playing.
Love is like beautiful flowers growing in the meadow.
Love is everybody's hearts.
Love is shiny, like shining stars.

Cally Blake (8)
Kingswood Junior School, Basildon

Angry

I feel like a bomb about to explode
My anger explosive like fireworks.

Bells ringing in my ears,
Like lightning hitting on a tree.

I feel like a fizzy bottle
About to fizz everywhere.

Callum Bowring (10)
Kingswood Junior School, Basildon

Love

Love is like the sense of a dove
Love smells like dreamy perfume just coming out of a bottle
Love feels like jumping onto cloud number 9
Love tastes like chocolate brownies coming out of the oven
Love sounds like a dove cooing in the field
Love looks like red roses blooming in the field
Love sounds like children laughing in the breeze
Love is light blue like bluebells.

Savani Kale (8)
Kingswood Junior School, Basildon

Pain

Red is the colour of pain, the fiery flames burning houses down one by one.
Pain tastes like flaming hot Monster Munch.
It smells of a pool full of rotten bones.
It sounds like a huge dog barking.
Pain feels like a war between two armies.
It looks like a soldier getting shot.
It reminds me of getting beaten up by a bunch of bullies.

Josh Grayer (9)
Kingswood Junior School, Basildon

Sadness

Sadness looks like a poorly paw on a puppy.
Sadness sounds like a teardrop rolling down a baby's cheek.
Sadness feels like the blue raindrops on your hand.
Sadness tastes like the dripping sad water.
Sadness is the colour of the sky on a rainy day.
Sadness smells like pouring water.

Jodie Bland (8)
Kingswood Junior School, Basildon

Baby Sister

In the hospital, my sister lying there -
Newborn - the happiest day of my life.

Cute, sweet as strawberries.
How pleased I was - a new sister.

She's older now, sweet as can be.
The way she takes her dummy out and kisses me.
I'm so lucky that I have a sister like her.

Faith Everett (9)
Kingswood Junior School, Basildon

Worry

Worry tastes like dirty water coming out of the pipes and
rotten food.
Worry is like you're uncomfortable and you can't stop moving
about and you feel sad.
The colour of worry is dark and dull colours.
Worry looks like sharp teeth like a crocodile and a pointy castle.
Worry smells like dying flowers in the garden and people smoking.

Zoe Allman (7)
Kingswood Junior School, Basildon

Enraged

The jangling of bells drills its way into my head,
as red blocks up my vision, enraging me further.
The smell of burning gases creates an excruciating taste.
The bells stop. It goes dark.
The cold falls as though it is drowning me.
Then, suddenly, a burning pain in my forehead
feels as though my head is on fire.

Jack Potter (10)
Kingswood Junior School, Basildon

Anger

Anger is like burning cakes.
Anger looks like fire.
Anger tastes like burning cakes.
Anger feels like being beaten.
Anger smells like the flames from a fire.
Anger is as red as Mars.
Anger sounds like fire burning.

Kuhle Nobanya (8)
Kingswood Junior School, Basildon

Sadness

Sadness is the dullest of greys.
It is the stench of petrol, fresh from a lawnmower.
It sounds like a deafening drill from a building site.
Sadness tastes like horrible burnt toast.
It feels like rough, uninviting tree bark.
It looks like someone crying alone.
Sadness reminds me of salty tears, falling down my face.

Olivia Bond (11)
Kingswood Junior School, Basildon

Sadness

Sadness is like a wounded puppy,
It's tasteless, like ice,
A scream inside my heart.
Sadness is like an unhappy child,
Looking for a parent.
Its colour is dark grey,
Like a miserable cloud, ready to cry.

Oliver Stewart (10)
Kingswood Junior School, Basildon

Happiness

Happiness looks like people going to get a takeaway for their dinner.
Happiness feels like sitting on a swing, swinging high and low.
Happiness is the colour yellow, like the sunshine.
Happiness tastes like chips and beans.
Happiness smells like my mum cooking my lovely dinner.
Happiness sounds like a baby giggling.

Hannah Morris (8)
Kingswood Junior School, Basildon

Joy

Joy is like the light green grass swaying in the summer breeze.
Joy looks like a cute puppy lying by the fireplace.
Joy feels like you being tickled.
Joy smells of a cake that has just come out of the oven.
Joy is like you stroking a puppy.
Joy tastes like a chocolate cake that just came out of the oven.

Jack Evans (8)
Kingswood Junior School, Basildon

Happiness

Happiness is yellow, like the burning sun.
It smells like beautiful flowers, swaying in the breeze.
It sounds like baby birds singing to each other.
It reminds me of my favourite thing - my family!
Happiness tastes like melting chocolate.
It feels like a warm cosy bed, just for you!

Lauren Knell (9)
Kingswood Junior School, Basildon

Hot Summer

Hot summer, going to the beach.
Swimming in the sea, lucky me.
Happy to be there, but watch out for rocks!
Walking along, sweating in the hot sun, sweat dripping off me.
No water to pour over me
or ways to cool down.

Haydn Bamfield (9)
Kingswood Junior School, Basildon

Anger

Anger looks like a red, red face.
Anger sounds like a bullet coming out of a gun.
Anger feels like someone punching you.
Anger smells like rotten eggs.
Anger tastes like Brussels sprouts.
Anger is red for fire that burns on wood.

Ben Campbell (8)
Kingswood Junior School, Basildon

Anger

Anger is like red hot lava.
Anger looks like a volcano erupting.
Anger sounds like someone screaming.
Anger feels like a hot kettle.
Anger tastes like mouldy mushrooms.
Anger smells like dusty gas.

Harrison Essam (8)
Kingswood Junior School, Basildon

Happiness

Happiness looks like the beautiful sun.
Happiness feels like the daisies' flower petals dropping
on your hand.
Happiness tastes like chocolate bunnies that you eat for Christmas.
Happiness smells like the red shiny roses.
Happiness sounds like the ducks flapping in the water.

Olivia Fitzpatrick (7)
Kingswood Junior School, Basildon

Love

Love is yellow like the rising sunlight.
Love is like flowers that grow up so bright.
Love sounds like bluebirds singing in a tree.
Love smells of my mum when she hugs me.
Love tastes of chocolate hearts flowing around us.
Love feels like soft pillows or a cat's soft cuddly fur covering you.

Natasha Rael (8)
Kingswood Junior School, Basildon

Sadness

Sadness feels like your heart breaking into a thousand pieces.
Sadness is like black and grey turning into a tornado.
Sadness looks like a bad person trying to hurt you.
Sadness sounds like thunder crashing down.
Sadness tastes like a rotten egg.
Sadness smells like hunters trying to hunt animals.

Isabel Buncher (8)
Kingswood Junior School, Basildon

Little Brother

E very day you cheer me up, even when I'm crying!
L iving with the best boy, cute, cuddly, friendly.
L ovely little brother, you bring joy to me.
I love you little brother, you are very cute.
  I feed you your bottle and you fall asleep.
S ometimes you laugh, I laugh and everyone laughs too!

Jasmine North (9)
Kingswood Junior School, Basildon

Worry

Worry is pitch-black like midnight.
Worry is the only living thing down your road.
Worry sounds like footsteps and screaming coming closer to you.
Worry smells like a gas plant that has leaked.
Worry tastes like bitter bread that has been left out too long.
Worry feels like a raging rabbit with rabies, biting you.

Nathan Cano-Lopez (8)
Kingswood Junior School, Basildon

Sadness

Sadness is dull, dark, deep.
Sadness looks like a person who's dropped dead.
Sadness sounds like guns all around me.
Sadness feels like you have let your dog go and die.
Sadness smells like dirty dull socks and old mouldy sausages.
Sadness tastes like you have last night's spaghetti.

Holly Ann Morrish (8)
Kingswood Junior School, Basildon

Sadness

Sadness is like your heart bursting.
Sadness sounds like the rain coming down.
Sadness smells like a tasty strawberry.
Sadness looks like chocolate cake and chocolate custard.
Sadness is when a baby cries.
Sadness is like you leaving school.

Brooke Macvicar (8)
Kingswood Junior School, Basildon

Love

Love is pink like a rose.
Love looks like a huge circle.
Love sounds like lovely music.
Love feels like a very smooth stone.
Love smells like fabulous air freshener.
Love tastes like chocolate.

Riley Shaw (8)
Kingswood Junior School, Basildon

Love

Love feels like a snuggly cuddle hug from my mum.
Love sounds like my mum singing in my garden.
Love smells like a lovely flower.
Love tastes like chocolate.
Love looks like a nice juicy strawberry.
Love is the colour of a red rose.

Chloe Macvicar (8)
Kingswood Junior School, Basildon

Love

Love sounds like a giggle from a baby.
Love feels like a big cuddle from my mum.
Love is the colour of a red, juicy strawberry.
Love tastes like a glass of juice going into my mouth.
Love smells like Febreeze.
Love looks like my family right there with me.

Millie Dawson (7)
Kingswood Junior School, Basildon

Anger

Anger feels like a charging rhino coming towards you.
Anger smells like toxic gas ascending your nostrils.
Anger looks like the slithery snakes on a gorgon's head.
Anger tastes of burning fire on your tongue.
Anger is like an enormous grey rhino bending its head down.
Anger is like red, boiling lava melting your house to smithereens.

Lewis Bunce (8)
Kingswood Junior School, Basildon

Puppies I Like

Puppies I like have smooth fur and little noses.
I love it when they chase me around the room.
Once one gets me, I'm sure it'll lick me.
They make me happy, joyful too.
Best of all their cute eyes, a cute smile as well;
But I mostly like them sleeping with me.

Coel Sharp (9)
Kingswood Junior School, Basildon

Sadness

Sadness looks like looking into my puppy's eyes.
Sadness is like sour sweets in your mouth.
Sadness sounds like your heart not beating.
Sadness smells like bad chocolate.
The colour of sadness is grey.

Maddie MacLeod (8)
Kingswood Junior School, Basildon

Joy

Joy looks like the sunset with hills, up and up, then down.
It sounds like a newborn baby, like the sound of classical music.
Joy feels like a tender skin coming from her mother's face.
It tastes like . . . a cookie . . . just coming out of the oven.
Joy smells like a spongy cake coming to get ready for a wedding.

Adesola Faniyi (8)
Kingswood Junior School, Basildon

Love

Love feels as nice as bed.
Love looks like a puppy's kiss.
Love sounds like a baby crying.
Love smells like shampoo.
Love tastes like nice roses.

Sam Francis (8)
Kingswood Junior School, Basildon

Worry

Worry is like the dark night.
Worry looks like the dark clouds.
Worry is like four really extremely dark colours.
Worry is mostly like a dark street.
Worry sounds like a wolf roaring at you.

Alfie Fisher (8)
Kingswood Junior School, Basildon

Happy

I feel as happy as a rabbit bouncing along the beautiful field.
Smelling the baking bread from the cottage at the top of the hill,
Listening to buzzing bees and fluttering butterflies,
And tasting the chocolate that makes me dribble.
Happy, it is the best feeling in the world.

Nishita Gadi (10)
Kingswood Junior School, Basildon

My Horse Is A Dream

She gallops along by the sea, daytime till noon.
Her tail dances in the breeze,
Her mane blowing beautifully.
Her shadow on the moon,
To me she is a dream come true.

Ella Maginn (9)
Kingswood Junior School, Basildon

Worry

Worry feels like lonely people in the playground.
Worry look like rain on a wet day.
Worry smells like gunpowder in the air.
Worry is the colour of pitch-black in the night sky.
Worry is the colour of dark blue in the evening.

Daniel Lambart (8)
Kingswood Junior School, Basildon

Anger

Anger is the colour black, blacker than space.
Anger feels like being trapped in a small cage that's burning in fire.
Anger sounds like people about to die.
Anger smells like rotting flesh and bodies.
Anger tastes like baby sick.

Willow Legg (7)
Kingswood Junior School, Basildon

Love

Love is light red like roses.
Love is like the most beautiful dog in the world.
Love is like the taste of chocolate.
Love is like the smell of roses.

Emma Murton (7)
Kingswood Junior School, Basildon

Anger

Anger looks like a raging volcano ready to spew out molten lava.
Anger feels like an alligator snapping at your feet.
Anger sounds like an evil cackle echoing through the streets.
Anger tastes like rotting fruit that you only picked yesterday.

Theo Stedman-Redican (8)
Kingswood Junior School, Basildon

Mummy

Mummy oh Mummy I love you.
Kisses and cuddles I get from you.
Treats and sweets come from you.
Mummy oh Mummy I love you.

Daisy Brunt (8)
Kingswood Junior School, Basildon

World Cup Fever

The time has come,
It's World Cup fun.
Everyone get ready,
Get the ball steady.
Lots of different countries taking part,
All with winning in their heart.
All the crowd will cheer,
While drinking lots of beer.
South Africa is the host,
But I hope they hit the post.
Come on England you can do it,
Put on your kit and let's get to it.

Charlie Wright (9)
Little Thurrock Primary School, Grays

Fisherman's Hook

We fish in the world seas
Chasing countless millions
To feed the hungry mouth
Spreading out nets far and wide
Trying to snare our prey

Don't think of us as evil
We fish to survive
I am a fisherman, smart I am
Sailing the seven seas, doing it for the best
With a boat and net I will catch my prey

I sat with my rod
With my courage by me
I felt a tug
Pulled by a hook came a stingray

I saw in its eyes what was happening
I knew I was guilty but work's work
My heart was heavy
I saw it had a few companions
Small, identical, they were babies
I cringed as I looked
She looked at me as she sat helplessly

I let her and its companions go
I was a second too late
That moment will sit on my heart forever
A monster I am.

Bradley Jones (11)
Little Thurrock Primary School, Grays

As I Walked . . .

As I walked down the rocky valley,
Rocky valley, rocky valley,
I saw a lion in the alley,
Hello, hello, hello.

Ring a jig-jog and away we go,
Way we go, way we go,
Ring a jig-jig and away we go,
Hello, hello, hello.

As I walked past the shimmering lake,
Shimmering lake, shimmering lake,
I saw a fish that was fake,
Hello, hello, hello.

As I walked through the shady park,
Shady park, shady park,
I saw a tree without any bark,
Hello, hello, hello.

As I walked down the road with a curl,
Road with a curl, road with a curl,
I met a crying and sobbing girl,
Hello, hello, hello.

As I came to the end of the Earth,
End of the Earth, end of the Earth,
I met a sun that was worth . . .
Some luck, some luck, some luck.

Esme Lucking (9)
Little Thurrock Primary School, Grays

Fisherman's Hook

We fish in the world's seas.
Chasing countless millions,
To feed the hungry mouths,
Spreading our nets far and wide.
Trying to snare our prey.

We catch salmon, cod, jellyfish and others,
We have friends, that we fish with,
Fishing alone to catch fish for the family,
With rods to catch and knives to chop.

I drift ahead to catch the fish and hear the waves crashing again,
I lower the rod,
That hooks to the jellyfish's mouth,
Then I realise it tries to swim away,
So I quickly pull it back again towards the shore.

Pulling it close and closer,
It struggles to swim away,
Its body turns around and around,
As I pull it to dry sand.

The jellyfish took its last breath,
As she gave birth to three babies,
The mother and her babies couldn't survive,
While blood trickled down her face,
I now have regrets.

Tommy Mason (11)
Little Thurrock Primary School, Grays

Casting A Hook

Today I am out by myself,
It's my duty too.
I earn a living,
By casting a hook,
By casting a hook,
I live in a world of regret.
We kill, we eat,
Just to survive.
You should know I don't like it,
I think I've caught a big one,
Don't worry,
They're cold-blooded, it doesn't hurt.
I do it by
Casting a hook,
By casting a hook.
I live in a world of regret,
We kill, we eat,
Just to survive.
A tear is trickling down my face.

Isabella Martin (10)
Little Thurrock Primary School, Grays

The Cheese

The cheese, the cheese,
The lonely yellow cheese sitting in the fridge,
All alone,
Crying all day and crying all night,
Sitting alone in the fridge,
Freezing cold.

Daniel Tagg (8)
Little Thurrock Primary School, Grays

I Love Music

Classical
Jazz
Rock and
Pop
I love music

Strings
Woodwind
Brass and
Percussion
Sections of the orchestra

Piano
Forté
Legato and
Staccato
Soft, loud, smooth and short

I love music.

Leoni Pring (10)
Little Thurrock Primary School, Grays

Family And Flowers!

My name is Rose and I live in a hose
I have a big nose and lovely fat toes
My mum is dumb and she has a big bum
My dad is fat with a rat in his hat
My sister is fat when she sits on a rat
But most of all we like the . . .
Flowers in the sky and
The flowers up high
The flowers all around
And there's some on the ground so
I picked some up with a lovely pound.

Caitlan Matthews (9)
Little Thurrock Primary School, Grays

The Shadow!

The shadow! The shadow!
Stretching everywhere,
Touching your toes, making you shiver,
The shadow! The shadow!
Giving goose bumps all over your arms.
The shadow! The shadow!
Growing bigger every night,
Haunting you until sunrise.
The shadow! The shadow!
Climbing up the walls until the room is pitch-black,
The shadow! The shadow!
Dark and gloomy making you feel petrified every night.
The shadow! The shadow!
Creeping in the night!
Ohhhh!

Alicia Bridge (9)
Little Thurrock Primary School, Grays

Window Race

Go little raindrop go!
Speeding down the window,
The cold, glinting window,
The unmoving droplets in the way,
My nose pressed against the glass,
Making it go misty.
I can't see my one now,
Is it winning, nobody knows.
Mine won, Mum's lost.
We'll do it again,
But only until the rain stops.

Hannah Phillips (9)
Little Thurrock Primary School, Grays

The River

    The river is
      a
   crowd
      surging
      and shoving
     its way
        to
    the exit
It trips
    and
tumbles and
 violently
  crashes
     against
    the rocks.

Hannah Obie (9)
Little Thurrock Primary School, Grays

Galaxy

The taste of chocolate,
Sticky and gooey,
Getting more scrummy,
More and more yummy.
Is this a dream?
A sleep in my bed?
No!
Don't go!
Goodbye creamy wonderland,
It's gone,
Forever.

Olivia Burns (10)
Little Thurrock Primary School, Grays

Sometimes

Sometimes I feel like there's nothing to be found
There's nothing for me to do
Just nothing
He leaves us in silence
Not a word
Quiet
Silence
Hear nothing
Unwelcoming feeling
Sometimes I cry
A tear running down my face
The coldness
There is nothing
Just a blank page
Whiteness.

Molly Johnson (9)
Little Thurrock Primary School, Grays

Water

Come with me
To the sea
And bring a rod
And we will catch some cod
Then we go for a swim
Look at that fish's fin
Look at the water
It reminds me of my daughter
Did you see that wave?
And you know my name is Dave.

Scott Regan (11)
Little Thurrock Primary School, Grays

An Egyptian Tale

In the white-hot desert sands
An ancient Egyptian pyramid stands
And deep inside you'll be sure to find
Cleopatra's statue when she was blind.
Walk a mile
And you will be sure to reach the river Nile.
Carry some Lynx
As you head to the sphinx.
Walk into the tomb
And find the secret room.
The mummy
Only comes out when it is sunny.
Wherever you move there will be a clue
Right next to you.
Look up in the sky
Then you will see Ra fly!

Nitin Chatrath (8)
Luton Junior School, Chatham

World Cup

Penalty kicker
Goal scorer
Great keeper
Excellent striker
Fast runner
Crazy tackler
Fantastic defender
Card giver
Crowd pleaser.

**Stephanie Southgate (7), Rayjay Haswell,
Harry Neill, Jake Carroll, Jake Mockford (8),
Brunthavan Ratnasingham (9) & Lucas Harvat (11)**
Luton Junior School, Chatham

Egypt

In the white-hot desert sands
An ancient Egyptian pyramid stands
And deep inside you'll be sure to find . . .
A man saying
Look at this soft sandy land
Then look at this tomb
With a magic room
Come with me to the river Nile
It will be over there in two miles
We're here, there's Jeremiad by the pyramid.

Stephanie Southgate (7)
Luton Junior School, Chatham

Dogs

A meat eater
A fast runner
A bone chaser
A high jumper
A good trainer
A fantastic digger
A lovely drinker.

Charlotte Lewis (8)
Luton Junior School, Chatham

Rat

I live in a chimney
I eat cheese
I come out at night
What am I?

A: Rat.

John Sawyer (8)
Luton Junior School, Chatham

Trapeze

T errifying
R eally good actions
A mazing
P erfect
E xciting
Z ealous
E xpect a lot.

Jessica Buckley (8)
Luton Junior School, Chatham

Footballer

A good scorer.
A ball stopper.
An excellent kicker.
A fantastic tackler.
What am I?

A footballer!

Tommy Barfoot (8)
Luton Junior School, Chatham

Me

A pain maker.
A trombone lover.
A saxophone player.
A bird hater.
What am I?

I am Keziah!

Keziah Dakat (8)
Luton Junior School, Chatham

Teacher

Tea slurper
High jumper
Tea lover
Big moaner
Getting older
Fruit lover.

Jake Carroll (8)
Luton Junior School, Chatham

Cat

Loves fish
Loves to sleep
Loves to play
Loves food
Loves drinking.

Emily Ager (8)
Luton Junior School, Chatham

Teachers

Tea drinker
Reflection giver
Cool talker
Ordinary walker.

Ellie James (8)
Luton Junior School, Chatham

Buzzing Bees

Bees buzzing around a flower,
Stay away, they have stinging power.
I bet you any kind of money,
That they're off now to make some honey.

Ellie Cooper (7)
Luton Junior School, Chatham

My Friend

A dam is my friend
D elightful man
A lways there
M emory of the class.

Brandon Richards (8)
Luton Junior School, Chatham

If

If I was a flower
that would give me the power
to make the world brighter
but I would have to be a fighter.

Alex Newman (7)
Luton Junior School, Chatham

Spiders - Haiku

Spiders are creepy . . .
Spiders are creepy-crawlies . . .
I really hate them!

Brooke Sandwell (8)
Luton Junior School, Chatham

Spring - Haiku

New lambs are skipping.
Children eating chocolate.
Bluebells start to bud.

Bradley Harris (7)
Luton Junior School, Chatham

Summer - Haiku

Sun is shining bright
It is time to splat suncream
Then put on your hat.

Olivia Cox (8)
Luton Junior School, Chatham

Spring - Haiku

I love spring so much
Someone likes to bring a song
The grass always waves.

Molly Fray (8)
Luton Junior School, Chatham

Summertime - Haiku

Have some ice cream now.
Get your cool sunglasses out.
Summertime is here!

Charlotte O'Gallagher (8)
Luton Junior School, Chatham

Spring - Haiku

Spring, spring, doorbells ring.
Everybody starts to sing.
Children like to swing.

Amy Geoghegan (8)
Luton Junior School, Chatham

Summertime - Haiku

Summer, you sunbathe
Let's get our swimming pool out
Summer is the best.

Joseph Petty (8)
Luton Junior School, Chatham

Dog

Brown eyes looking at me,
Puppy ears and a waggly tail,
He runs round in circles
Like a spinning wheel.

Sometimes he is quiet,
Sometimes he is mad,
And when he's mad he jumps up and down,
But when he is quiet,
He makes me feel peaceful.

His furry body is like a soft blanket
And I can bury my face in it
And forget about everything.

Tim Gilbey (11)
Moreton Hall Preparatory School, Bury St Edmunds

Election Time

Everyone it's election time,
Everyone it's time to rhyme!
Who will you vote for
To stay behind No 10 door?

Will it be Nick Clegg?
He can rule big and meg!
He can also be quite funny
Although he wants to change our money!

Will it be Gordon Brown?
He would never let you drown.
We've had him before,
And he can be a bit of a bore!

Will it be David Cameron?
He is great at cooking hameron!
He wants to control immigration,
But that would be bad for the nation!

So now cast your vote,
But please do note;
That whoever you vote for,
Might end up behind No 10 door!

Issy Rush (11)
Moreton Hall Preparatory School, Bury St Edmunds

Politics

Have you seen that Gordon Brown?
He does not have a clue!
All he really says all day is,
'I will change the economy for you!'

Have you seen that Gordon Brown?
He really makes me sad.
All the time he wants to frown,
What a boring lad!

Have you seen that Gordon Brown?
He could not lead a school.
I'd hate him as the headmaster,
I bet he's really cruel.

Have you seen that David Cameron?
He's the ruler of the *land!*
That's why he's the Prime Minister,
And Gordon Brown is banned.

Have you seen that David Cameron?
He really makes me smile.
He's changing the economy,
I hope he's the leader for a while.

Have you seen that David Cameron?
I think he's very cool.
He makes the right decisions,
Unlike that other fool.

Oliver Heazel (11)
Oakfields Montessori School, Upminster

Wild West

There's a place where the streets are dusty,
Where the folks' party spirit never dies,
Where the men spit into small tin cans,
And the sun is high in the sky.

I'm talking about the Wild West,
Home to all the young cowboys,
It's a place where the bars are always full,
And the air where the bald eagles fly.

There's a place where the men are wild,
Where they stare at each other in the eyes,
Then they count to a certain number,
Then they turn, *bang!* One then dies.

I'm talking about the Wild West,
It's a place where men are bold,
Where the streets are filled with gunfire,
And the 'yee hars' never grow old!

I love the spirit of the ol' Wild West,
It's a cowboy's dusty heaven,
Now I have to go back to my home,
Cos Mum's cooking dinner at seven!

Adam Williams (11)
Oakfields Montessori School, Upminster

My Bloomin' Cactus

Out of all the cacti that I own,
The bloomin' one's the best,
With the 1 foot flower that has grown,
It's really quite a pest.

It sits upon my window sill,
Hogging all the light,
The score is bloomin' 1, other 0,
It's really quite a fright.

The cactus blooms a flower,
But only for a day,
It takes up all its power,
Then it shrivels and fades away.

I really like my bloomin' plant,
It's bigger than itself,
I want to hug it, but I simply can't,
It'll prickle me, very bad for my health.

Out of all the cacti that I own,
The bloomin' one's the best,
With the 1 foot flower that has grown,
It beats all the cacti tests.

Beth Wilson (11)
Oakfields Montessori School, Upminster

My Brother!

My brother is a monster
When he's munching his food
And when he loses a life on dig dug
He gets into a mood.

When he's in a mood
He goes and gets a ball
And when he goes outside
He kicks it at the wall.

When he's kicking the ball
My mum goes mad
And when he comes in
He calls my mum bad!

When he goes to school
He picks on everyone
And when he picks on one of the boys
He throws the table!

When he's at the park
He goes crazy
And when he sits down
He's very lazy!

Ellie Healy (9)
Oakfields Montessori School, Upminster

The Monster Down The Drain

The monster down the drain
Sucks up all the rain

It's as slimy as snails
It has four tails

It is as rusty as nails
And breathes out gales

It is as cheeky as a monkey
It is fat and chunky

When it comes
You hear banging on drums

It has warts on its toes
And feathers around its nose

It sleeps in a cot
And eats from a pot

It cries
When it tries

Be careful of this beast
You might be its next feast.

Morgan Miles (8)
Oakfields Montessori School, Upminster

Running
(In the style of Wendy Cope)

I like sports
I am very fond of running.

I like running
I am very fond of sports.

I am sports of running
I like very fond.

A fond sports of 'I like, I am' -
Very running.

Fond of 'like I running?
Am I? - a very sports'.

Running of a sports!
Am I fond? Like I very?

Sports running! I like
I am fond of a 'very'.

I am of very fond running
Like I a sports?

Bethany Bradley (11)
Oakfields Montessori School, Upminster

Imagination

Imagination,
It's all in your head,
An amazing fantasy world,
That is found inside your bed.

Imagination,
Creating heroes,
Beating baddies across the world,
Before turning them back into zeroes.

Imagination,
Sometimes can be bad,
But it's all a cunning deception,
Because you wake up and you're still a lad.

Imagination,
You can be a super sensation,
But even your normal self has a power,
The power of imagination.

Ben Kinder (11)
Oakfields Montessori School, Upminster

At The Beach

The waves splashing all over the place
The sand swishing around
Sandcastles all over the place
Beach towels all around
People lying down
Beautiful views all over the place
It is really fun.

Layla Choudhury (9)
Oakfields Montessori School, Upminster

My Sister

My sister thinks she is cute
But I say she's not
I wish she would fall in our dinner
And we can eat her in the pot
She's always arguing with me
She's so annoying
She's a monster in disguise
Her fingers are crooked in all different ways
Her eyes are red like devils' eyes
Her teeth are like gravestones
You see she is a devil in disguise.

Sophie Gilkes-Tarsey (8)
Oakfields Montessori School, Upminster

Robots

They are square
They are small
They are very, very tall.

There are dinosaur robots
There are killer robots.

They are dumb
They are smart
They have three thumbs.

Robots are cool
Robots are not cool
Some are actually a fool.

Robots are machines with what a grip
They are strong or weak
Watch out!
They could embarrass you by pulling your trouser zip!

Zain Ansari (9)
Oakfields Montessori School, Upminster

My Sister

My sister is a monster
My sister is a devil
My sister was born down on the fourth level

She may look sweet
But she is no treat
Look at the green spots on her feet

She is as ugly as a pig
She is really quite big
She is bald so wears a wig

She is a devil in disguise.

Henry O'Leary (9)
Oakfields Montessori School, Upminster

My Brother The Devil

My brother is the Devil
He has two red pointed ears
And a torch in case someone appears
He might look sweet but he is a devil

He's as grumpy as a bull
If you go near him he will kill you in one shot
He shoots fireballs out of his eyes
It will burn you to dust
What a surprise.

Patrick Mulroy-Yourell (9)
Oakfields Montessori School, Upminster

The Silver Moon

When I look up at the silver moon,
I remember my mother's heart-warming smile,
The warmth of her arms around me,
The breeze of her breath on my brow,
And I want her to be with me now . . .

When I look up at the silver moon,
I forget the many times,
My rebel ways or cheekiness
That had made my mother frown,
And I want her to be with me now . . .

From beyond the moon, beyond the stars . . .
Beyond the deep, deep glistening sky,
My mother calls to me each night,
'Raman, I am here.'
And I call back, 'So am I.'

Raman Aval (11)
Oakfields Montessori School, Upminster

Friends

A friend is like a flower,
a rose to be exact.

A friend is like a caterpillar -
growing into a butterfly,
or maybe like a brand new gate
that never comes unattached.

A friend is like a heart
that never stops beating.

Emily Gilkes-Tarsey (11)
Oakfields Montessori School, Upminster

Football
(In the style of Wendy Cope)

I like sport.
I'm very fond of football.

I'm football.
I'm very fond of a sport.

I'm sports of football.
I like very fond of sports.

Fond of 'like I football?'
Am I? - A very sports.

Fond of football I am, I am.
Very football indeed.

I'm very fond football.
Am I a sport?

Michael Wenman (11)
Oakfields Montessori School, Upminster

My Monster!

Every night I go to bed,
I see a figure pass,
Its gleaming eyes stare at me,
No matter where I glance.

Its eyes are like cats,
His claws are like pins,
His razor-sharp teeth
And his black, black skin.

Well the monster's gone,
What a relief,
But now there's another,
And he gives me grief.

Mia Choudhury (10)
Oakfields Montessori School, Upminster

Disco!

I went to a disco
Everyone was there
I bought some drinks from the bar
I got drunk and fell off the chair.
I was dancing on the dance floor
The DJ pumped up his hair
I gave him a song about a thong
That my mum always wears.
I got up onto the stage
Told a joke
No one laughed
It made me choke.
It wasn't the joke
I had an out-of-date burger
I left the disco and didn't take it any further.

Rachel Harvey (8)
Oakfields Montessori School, Upminster

My Pet

My dog is coming, she's not here yet,
Her name is Maggie, she will be my pet.
A basket and bowl, I need to get.
When she comes, she'll have been to the vet.

My dog is coming, she's not here yet,
She's soft and furry, black as jet.
Her tongue is pink, her eyes are brown,
Time feels long when she's not around.

Emily Edinburgh (9)
Oaklands School, Loughton

Cats

Cats, cats everywhere,
Cats chewing on my hair,
Cats tearing up the stairs,
Bird feathers everywhere.

Cats, cats everywhere,
Cats swinging on my shoulder,
I hope they won't do this when they're older!

Cats, cats everywhere,
A tabby one and a Burmese Blue,
I can't believe we just have two!

Elizabeth Davis (9)
Oaklands School, Loughton

My Pony

My pony is a dappled grey,
She loves to jump and play.
My pony is a dappled grey,
I see her every day.

My pony has some shiny tack,
It shimmers in the sun.
My pony has some shiny tack,
My work is never done.

Isabella Singer (9)
Oaklands School, Loughton

My Cat

My cat is black and white,
I snuggle up with him tight,
My love for him is so strong,
Even though he does pong!

He is called Tom the cat,
He curls up on a furry mat,
Even when he stains the carpet,
I'll buy him a new one from the market.

He chases birds, dogs and flies,
Down the road and up The Rise,
Even though he is annoying,
All the family enjoy him.

But that's just him -
My cat!

Holly Hembury (8)
Oaklands School, Loughton

Beach

The beach looks like a shiny sapphire in a gold setting.
It feels like you're sitting on a golden pillow.
The beach is a shiny baby blue like the sky.
It tastes like an ice cream with strawberry cream.
It smells of a beautiful red rose.
It reminds me of Kidspace but more fun.

Kayla Stone (9)
St Joseph's RC Primary School, Barking

Growing Up

Growing up reminds me of a tiny seed,
transformed into a great big tree.

Growing up feels like a rusty caterpillar,
transforming into a smooth velvet butterfly.

Growing up sounds like fun,
but not when all the work needs to be done.

Growing up tastes like dark chocolate,
sweet but bitter in its own way.

Growing up smells like a sweet perfume,
free to smell but dear to buy.

Growing up looks like a tall big tree,
shrinking to become an old forgotten stump.

Growing up is like having your beautiful black hair
changing to become all so grey.

Chantel-Marie Atayi (10)
St Joseph's RC Primary School, Barking

Autumn

Autumn is a cold month
It smells like pure nature
It's orange like the setting sun
It reminds me of cold winter.

It has a strong smell of air
It makes blossom on trees
It feels like air
It sounds like air
It tastes like air.

Elson Simoni (10)
St Joseph's RC Primary School, Barking

The Future

The future looks like colourful flowers and beautiful butterflies twinkling in the beaming sun.
The future feels warm like a furry bear's cuddle.
The future tastes like a spring cake flying past you.
Future is a colour that you can't even imagine.
The future smells like flowers exploding into the air.
The future reminds me of best friends playing around in the summer grass.
Future sounds like sheep going *ba-aa-aa* and horses going *nay-yy*.

Eimear Browne (10)
St Joseph's RC Primary School, Barking

Time

Time tastes like your favourite sweets,
Time sounds like a hundred heart beats,
Time feels like sand slipping through your fingers,
Time smells like perfume that lingers.
Time reminds you of fun with your best friend,
Time looks like the world's at its end.
Time is all the colours of the rainbow but best of all . . .
Time will never go!

Cristina Mascia (10)
St Joseph's RC Primary School, Barking

Happiness

Happiness reminds me of summer beaches.
Happiness sounds like hyenas laughing.
Happiness tastes like eating chocolate.
Happiness is like a yellow daffodil coming up.
Happiness is like the smell of a barbecue.

Laurynas Neverauskas (10)
St Joseph's RC Primary School, Barking

Wonder

Wonder is like getting lost in a dreamy dream.
Wonder feels like being carried by a handsome prince.
Wonder looks like a magical illusion.
Wonder looks like angels flying above.
Wonder reminds me of eating chocolate cake and getting lost in it.
Wonder tastes like ice cream with sprinkles on top.
Wonder looks like paint thrown on the wall.
Last of all, wonder is like a newborn baby.

Paula Matovu (9)
St Joseph's RC Primary School, Barking

Evening

Evening smells like nature.
Evening feels like the world comes together as one.
Evening is a time to relax to enjoy your family to reflect on your beautiful day.
Evening is as beautiful as the sunset.
Evening reminds me of the day my cousin was born, everyone was happy.
Evening tastes like a million sweets on your tongue.

Arthur Anyanjo (10)
St Joseph's RC Primary School, Barking

Fun

Fun is as colourful as a rainbow floating at midday.
Fun looks like two friends playing in the sun.
It smells like a warm breeze in the air.
It feels like a smooth surface on a beach.
It sounds like laughter in the playground.
It tastes like ice cream with a cherry on top.

Dylan Nirde (10)
St Joseph's RC Primary School, Barking

Forest

It smells of fresh air and nice smelling flowers with the smell of the trees.
It looks like there are lots of streams and green and red trees.
It sounds like birds chirping and trees waving with streams streaming.
It tastes like fresh air coming into your mouth.
It reminds me of being in the country with my granddad and dog in the forest.

Emily Peace (10)
St Joseph's RC Primary School, Barking

Spring

Spring sounds like the new birds singing early in the morning.
Spring smells like a red rose just opening up.
Spring looks like a pink pearl lighting up the whole room.
Spring reminds me of baby animals just being born, waking up to the new smell of spring.
Spring feels like you're in a whole new world full of blossom.
Spring tastes like a load of sweets instead of blossom on trees.
Spring's colour is like a ripe red strawberry.

Jaden Toussaint (10)
St Joseph's RC Primary School, Barking

Anger

Anger is as red as burning fire
Anger smells like gas
Anger sounds like an evil laugh
Anger tastes like raw fish
Anger feels like an earthquake.

Kofi Agyeman Boamah (8)
St Joseph's RC Primary School, Barking

Winter

Winter sounds like falling snow, crushing down on the floor.
Winter smells like bitter heaps of herbs.
Winter reminds me of Christmas.
Winter tastes like freedom in the snow.
Winter feels like the cold side of happiness.
Winter looks white and pretty.
Winter's colour is white, big, soft and cuddly.

Darragh Wilson (10)
St Joseph's RC Primary School, Barking

Silence

Mute is as silent as the Pink Panther.
Silence tastes like a low fat bread.
Silence looks like the moon in the dark.
Silence feels like you are in a hot tub.
Silence sounds like a book with no pages.
Silence reminds you of being on your own, peacefully.
Silence is as black as a shadow.

Nathan Vitorino (10)
St Joseph's RC Primary School, Barking

Courage

Courage is purple like an exotic flower.
Courage feels like strength to keep you going.
Courage tastes like a fresh juicy orange.
Courage reminds me of St George killing the dragon.
Courage looks like the orangy red sunset.
Courage smells like a cinnamon candle burning through the night.
Courage sounds like someone saying sorry.

Linpaul Rodney (10)
St Joseph's RC Primary School, Barking

Change

Change looks like a new baby
Change reminds me of myself
Change looks different
Change sounds as deep as a grave
Change smells as awful as poo
Change tastes as funky as toilet water
Change is also a big giant.

Clayton Bokanga (9)
St Joseph's RC Primary School, Barking

Joy

Joy sounds like happiness.
Joy tastes like hot chicken wings.
Joy is red, light red.
Joy reminds me of the hottest place.
Joy smells of sweat.
Joy feels like that everyone likes you.
Joy looks like everyone giggling.

Rochelle McLaren (9)
St Joseph's RC Primary School, Barking

Journey

A journey is the smell of adventure awaiting you on your way.
A journey tastes like really sweet and sugary sweets.
A journey feels like a rumbly feeling inside your tummy.
A journey sounds like a gruffly sore throat on an ill person.
A journey reminds me of a funfair ride in the park.
A journey looks like the road is moving as fast as a cheetah.
A journey's colour is as bright as a polar bear in the North Pole.

Conor Jason (10)
St Joseph's RC Primary School, Barking

Morning

Morning sounds like a doorbell ringing.
Morning is like a dazzling, sparkly sky.
Morning smells like a bowl of cereals.
Morning reminds me of a brand new day.
Morning feels like roses fluttering in the sky.
Morning is the colour of crusty bacon.
Morning tastes like fried eggs.

Danielle Parker (9)
St Joseph's RC Primary School, Barking

Discovery

Discovery tastes like strawberries dipped in rich chocolate sauce.
Discovery feels like rich embroidered silk.
Discovery looks like a magical illusion.
Discovery smells like roses.
Discovery reminds you of the moment you were born.
Discovery sounds like the sweet sound of doves singing.
Discovery is the colour of rich, bright gold.

Oshi-Ada Idagu (10)
St Joseph's RC Primary School, Barking

Anger

Anger is dark, dripping, painful, bloody red.
Anger smells like a squashed dead rat.
Anger sounds like angry eagles chasing.
Anger tastes like spicy hot pepper.
Anger feels like dying in fire.

Carl King (8)
St Joseph's RC Primary School, Barking

Excitement

Excitement is sparkly like a disco ball.
Excitement smells like beautiful basil plants.
Excitement sounds like superb magpies singing.
Excitement tastes like a healthy sandwich.
Excitement feels like a newborn sweet baby.

Chloe Okerago (8)
St Joseph's RC Primary School, Barking

My Sense Poem: Anger

Anger is a black dark colour.
Anger tastes like hot spicy peppers.
Anger smells like choking smoke.
Anger feels like a shock of lightning.
Anger sounds like a fork screeching across my plate.

Ethan Dixon (8)
St Joseph's RC Primary School, Barking

Happiness

Happiness is bright ginger yellow.
Happiness smells like a red rose.
Happiness sounds like twittering birds.
Happiness tastes like sticky honey.
Happiness feels like a breeze of wind.

Elyas Ribeiro Cretu (7)
St Joseph's RC Primary School, Barking

Happiness

Happiness is as pretty as a sunny yellow rose.
Happiness smells like nature.
Happiness sounds like a little chick tweeting in the early morning.
Happiness tastes like the sweet Italian spicy pizza.
Happiness feels like a blowing breeze.

Dischan Mofaya Kimpini (7)
St Joseph's RC Primary School, Barking

Anger

Anger is as black as thunder in the sky.
Anger smells like burning hot fire.
Anger sounds like big waves crashing on some rocks.
Anger tastes like a red-hot chilli pepper.
Anger feels like a big spiky cactus.

Sharanya Kilbert (8)
St Joseph's RC Primary School, Barking

My Sense Poem - Anger

Anger looks like a black, dark, spooky room.
Anger smells like blood dripping down the hallway.
Anger sounds like hot burning fire.
Anger tastes like dirty dirt.
Anger feels like flashing, lashing lightning.

Callum Jason (8)
St Joseph's RC Primary School, Barking

Happiness

Happiness is a smiley yellow person.
Happiness smells like perfume.
Happiness sounds like the wind.
Happiness tastes like Nutella.
Happiness feels like candyfloss.

Mateusz Swiecicki (8)
St Joseph's RC Primary School, Barking

Anger

Anger is fiery red.
Anger smells like burnt toast.
Anger sounds like the waves crashing against rocks.
Anger tastes like spicy hot peppers.
Anger feels like a ball of hot fire.

Jade Flannery (8)
St Joseph's RC Primary School, Barking

Anger

Anger is dark bloody red.
Anger smells like the Devil's burning breath.
Anger sounds like a baby fox shrieking.
Anger tastes like a hot spicy chilli.
Anger feels like a big black bull stabbing you right in the back.

Harry Webster (8)
St Joseph's RC Primary School, Barking

Anger

Anger smells like burnt toast
Anger tastes like spicy hot pepper
Anger feels like a killed sheep
Anger sounds like roaring.

Suganya Kinslirobad (8)
St Joseph's RC Primary School, Barking

My Senses Poem

Anger looks like a house is on fire
Anger sounds like bursting thunder
Anger tastes like dusty dirt
Anger feels like hard black rock.

James Hunt (8)
St Joseph's RC Primary School, Barking

Cousins

My cousins are little and cute,
Some are big and annoying,
But I like them all the same,
They can love you like a brother or sister,
Or make you get the blame!

Elliott Glynn (8)
Skippers Hill Manor School, Mayfield

Latin Test

Tick-tock, tick-tock
Drip, drip, drip, drip
Scratch, scratch, scratch, scratch
'What does Pugno mean?'
The tension, the most uncomfortable thing ever
I forgot the answer
2 seconds and then the next question
N
  o
    o
      o
        o
          o it's too late
I am going to
            f
           a
          i
         l!
The next day;
'I will call out the names of people who have failed.
At the very bottom of the class is . . .
Issie.'
Noooo!

Isabelle Peach (10)
Skippers Hill Manor School, Mayfield

Charlie!

Charlie, well where do I begin? He has a smile, he has a grin
He crunches his food, he isn't rude, he isn't crude, he is perfectly perfect
He isn't blue, he isn't green, sometimes he's never even seen
He slurps his water, he doesn't burp, he doesn't speak like absurd parrots
He runs about, he makes a track, but he doesn't lose his utter grace
He'd definitely win a race
He's not a dog, he's not a cat, he's not a little annoying brat
He's not a bother, he's not an echo
Oh!
But did I mention, he's my gecko?

Amelia Field (10)
Skippers Hill Manor School, Mayfield

Little Bears

Bears are cute
Bears look cuddly
Bears are brown
But really they want to
Eat you!

Sarah Shepherd (8)
Skippers Hill Manor School, Mayfield

The Cat

Hunting through the garden
to impress his owner
slashing through
the bushes
then he
ducks
down
But all you can see is a
tall, fluffy tail
that is the sign
for any creature
to run.
Run, run, run little mouse!
But the large smile says
Say your last prayer
little mouse!
Munch! He's a gonner!
After that it's
back home
with his very
curly tail
swishing
and swirling.

Eliza Dunhill (10)
Skippers Hill Manor School, Mayfield

Months

January, back to school again, getting up early is a pain.
February, it is half-term, my cousins came over and saw a worm.
March, it is my mummy's birthday, 'Happy birthday,' I like to say.
April brings hail and showers, I love to see all the flowers.
May, the lambs spring and play, I'd love to watch them all day.
June, it is usually the start of the sun, I don't like to eat an iced bun.
July, it's the start of the summer holiday, the start of fun and play.
August usually is the hottest month of the year, I like to go to Brighton Pier.
September, it's a new year at school, my brother James jumps in the pool.
October, it's the crunchy leaves, Mummy has a receipt that she receives.
November, it's fireworks and bonfire night, let's hope the animals don't get a fright.
December, it's Christmas time, I like to eat fruit but not a lime!

Francesca Plaskett (7)
Skippers Hill Manor School, Mayfield

The Cliff Of Death

Wind rushes past your spine and wolves howl,
Screams from nowhere gather in the deadly night,
Ghostly figures creep around by the cliff of death.

Bloodstains glow scarlet red flashing continuously,
Spiders crawling in the silent moonlight and an evil face looking at you,
You close your eyes by the cliff of death.

A blood tipped sword stabbed into a gloomy tree,
The cliff shifts a step in the deadly night,
Then a scream and silence by the cliff of death.

Gabby Leach (9)
Skippers Hill Manor School, Mayfield

Granma

Is she nice, is she mean, is she very, very keen?
    Does she bring you presents?
Is she young, is she old, is she very, very cold?
    Is she funny?
Is she happy, is she sad, is she very, very glad?
    Are you friends?

My granma is nice and very, very keen, she is old,
she is happy, she does bring me presents,
she is very, very funny, we are friends, she is warm!
    I think my granma is brilliant!

Louisa Hurel (10)
Skippers Hill Manor School, Mayfield

Busy Animals

Wild bunnies clawing at the muddy ground
Digging tunnels to keep them safe and sound
Amazingly coloured birds flying through the bright blue sky
Soaring fast and going high
Beautiful dolphins jumping through the sparkling sea
Their dark grey faces are full of glee
Bright yellow ducklings swimming with their mum and dad
Paddling gracefully, looking glad
Animals doing something, anytime, anywhere
Hunting for food like the big fluffy bear.

Jessy Leach (9)
Skippers Hill Manor School, Mayfield

My Dog

My dog is called Fred
My dog loves to eat
My dog's favourite food is chicken in gravy
My dog is as fast as a fox
My dog can jump as high as a deer
My dog's claws are as sharp as a bear's
My dog is as small as a lamb
    My dog I love.

Oscar Steward (9)
Skippers Hill Manor School, Mayfield

Planes

Planes, planes, planes
I love planes
Planes here, planes there
I love planes

34,000 feet
450 miles per hour
I love planes.

Ben Leach (10)
Skippers Hill Manor School, Mayfield

Animals

A lice has an ant, he's already been squashed
N atalie has a newt, he's really, really tiny
I saac has an insect, he won't tell me what it is
M arella has a mouse, she has to munch cheese
A lice has just got another ant, this time it survived
L ucy has a leopard, he's really, really cute
S o I wonder what I should get.

Lizzie Webb (9)
Skippers Hill Manor School, Mayfield

Rugby

R ugby is as brilliant as chocolate, or better!
U se a ball big or small, squiggy and flat, or as hard as a rock.
G rubby, muddy, dirty brown like the leaves in the autumn
   with the sun shining on the horizon.
B roken arms and legs, 'You just stood on my finger!'
Y ou go past one, you go past two, you're in the clear.
   Poof! You're down.

Matthew Scates (9)
Skippers Hill Manor School, Mayfield

The Something

What is it?
It's there on the floor and it's left a slimy trail through the door.
It's oozing and goosing and throbbing and bobbing.
And . . . it's sneezed.
It's moving, it's climbing up my leg!
It bites me, it hits me, it throws me on the floor.
Now it's dragging me through the door.

Thomas Stone (10)
Skippers Hill Manor School, Mayfield

Spring Poem

When I go out
I really doubt that there is snow.
I'm glad about that!
I see the baby rats,
They're in their little hole,
No, it's a water hole.
Blossom falls from the trees,
I really do feel the breeze.
Daffodils sprout from the ground,
But it doesn't get trodden by a hound.
Wow! Look over there,
It's a bear.
'Run!' but I still like spring.

Jacob Robson (9)
The Heritage School, Cambridge

Spring Nature Poem

Spring has sprung,
It has begun,
I love to see its nature,
The blossom is white as snow,
The kingfisher sploshes and splashes,
Peck, peck, peck the woodpecker hits the beech tree,
I really love the spring,
It is so light.

William Buchanan (7)
The Heritage School, Cambridge

Spring Poem

Spring is here,
It brings some cheer,
Begs the eggs,
For baby beds.

Blossom comes,
With trees and leaves.
The breeze and bees,
Have lots of rays.

Birds have nests,
And that is best,
Chicks have come,
With the sun.
Rain has promised
That it will be honest.

Robert Carter (8)
The Heritage School, Cambridge

Daffodils

Daffodils,
daffodils,
as the blossom falls on you.

You are yellow
with green stalks
and are a great present
for Mother's Day.

Some people pick you single
and some people pick you in a bunch.

The daffodils are dead,
the spring has gone!
That doesn't matter
because I have ice cream.

Alex Keller (7)
The Heritage School, Cambridge

Spring Wildlife

Deer cries in early morning,
Echo through the brush,
Baby owlets sleeping,
So don't make a noise - *hush!*

Bunnies in the bluebells,
Their mothers digging holes,
Deer in the buttercups,
Antlers big and bold.

Birds are laying speckled eggs,
White, turquoise and blue,
Magpies come to steal them,
Unfortunate but true.

Jennifer Bell (8)
The Heritage School, Cambridge

Spring Poem

Spring has begun
Daffodils have come
Sun has begun
Baby birds have come
Ducklings have hatched

Eggs have come
Nests are made
Spring is beautiful
Rain has come
Nights are short
Days are long

Baby chicks are born in the light of the moon.

Olivia Alderson (7)
The Heritage School, Cambridge

Spring

Spring has sprung,
It has begun,
As the young birds are born,
Their parents call, 'Spring has begun.'

The baby ducklings take their first swim,
As the sun and rain meet,
A rainbow appears,
Everybody is happy,
Spring has appeared.

Oliver Chapman (8)
The Heritage School, Cambridge

The Kingfisher

The kingfisher flashes
The kingfisher dashes
The kingfisher gnashes
At his prey.

He feeds his young
Spring has begun
Off he goes again.

Seth Fletcher (8)
The Heritage School, Cambridge

Spring Poem

Spring, spring,
How beautiful you look,
Especially by the lovely brook.
Spring's springing,
Flowers singing,
Lovely spring,
Your bluebells ring.

Kane Blake (7)
The Heritage School, Cambridge

Spring The Love

'Are the spring flowers out yet?'
'Yes of course they are! Spring has come again.'
'Are the people still picking flowers?'
'Yes of course they are! We draw them with a pen.'
'Are flowers the best thing of all?'
'Yes of course they are!'
'They are always in the light!'

Joanna Haylett (8)
The Heritage School, Cambridge

Spring

Spring has sprung
Spring has begun
Begging for eggs
Begging birds to nest.

Flowers have sprung
Bees are buzzing.

Zachary Dampier-Kell (7)
The Heritage School, Cambridge

Lovely Spring

Spring has sprung
Winter is gone and done
It is fun and cheery
It is lovely
In the breeze
Flowers are cuddling.

Rosa Tate (7)
The Heritage School, Cambridge

Spring Poem

Baby chicks are born in the light,
The chicks are cute and soft.
They swim with their mother duck
In the light and dark.

Bradley McMahon (7)
The Heritage School, Cambridge

Spring Poem

In spring the blossom starts to grow!
It is as white as snow.
Blossom everywhere,
In fields, by the river and everywhere.

Catherine Smartt (7)
The Heritage School, Cambridge

Ladybird, Ladybird

Some live in long green grass.
All of them have patterns on their back.
These minibeasts have wings
But look like they don't have wings.
These creatures have black spots on their back that tell you their age.
Some minibeasts are yellow and black.
Some creatures have white and black eyes.
Spiders can kill them.
I like to hold a ladybird
Because it crawls around and tickles me.

Michael Maxted (7)
The Howbridge Infant School, Witham

What Am I?

Jump, jump, jump, jump,
We want to see you,
My camouflage is green
My name beings with G
My name is grasshopper
I live in the woods.

Grasshopper.

Funmilola Bamigbele (6)
The Howbridge Infant School, Witham

Spiders

Every spider spins sticky webs
Every spider has eight legs
Every spider eats other bugs
I like looking after different spiders
Every spider would eat their baby
Every spider scares lots of people
Every spider is a bit hairy
Really spiders are quite friendly
Every spider is a bit scary
Every spider runs very fast.

Thomas Miranda (7)
The Howbridge Infant School, Witham

Untitled

Ladybird, ladybird fly away home,
Your house is on fire,
Your children are gone.
Fly through the forest,
Get to your tree,
Your children are safe.
Bees fly south to east to one flower to another,
If they come buzzing to your head,
Here's some advice, just stand there
And it will go away.

Abbie Brown (7)
The Howbridge Infant School, Witham

What Am I?

Has 224 legs.
Has a hard shell and it has the shell across its back.
Curls up into a ball.
Its antennae tell it when it is day or night.
It runs really fast.
Has black eyes.
Has brown skin.

A centipede.

Ben Nixon (7)
The Howbridge Infant School, Witham

What Am I?

They are small and some are big
You should never step on them because they are very fragile
They curl up into a ball when predators are near
It might curl up in your hand because it is scared
Some are slow and some are fast
They are grey and they have 18 legs
They have tiny lines on their tiny grey shells.

Woodlouse.

Robyn Babbs (7)
The Howbridge Infant School, Witham

Untitled

Butterfly fly away,
Your wings are beautiful,
It's a lovely day.
The sun is out,
Butterfly your wings are colourful with pink spots on,
Your suit is camouflaged.

Emma Walsh (7)
The Howbridge Infant School, Witham

Cockroach

Cockroach look over there,
that person who has been bugging you and hurting you,
I think that you need to have a word with him
to get him to be nice to you
and get him to be gentle
then you won't get hurt
and he won't be unkind
and you could be friends.

Teddy Creasey (7)
The Howbridge Infant School, Witham

What Am I?

Some are hairy and scary
Some eat their babies
They spin webs to catch their prey
They have long legs
I like touching these
They all have eight legs.

They are spiders.

Ben Mawhood (6)
The Howbridge Infant School, Witham

Bees

Bees flying in the sky,
Yellow and black,
Flying in the sky with their wings open in the sunshine,
Trying to find people to sting.
They collect pollen to make honey.
Bees have wings to help them fly,
Bees look for pollen.

Fahima Uddin (7)
The Howbridge Infant School, Witham

Untitled

Bees, bees can sting
they hover and buzz
they like the flowers
and they can make sweet honey
really yummy
they are stripy and fierce
and very scary.

Baillie Mason (6)
The Howbridge Infant School, Witham

Untitled

A bug with a shiny shell
Some hiss, some don't
A bug that may have wings but some don't
There are lot of different types
Shall I tell you its name?
It's called a cockroach
Lots around the wood.

Billy Simmons (7)
The Howbridge Infant School, Witham

Butterfly

Symmetrical butterflies flying away
so beautiful, gentle and calm.
Sucking juice from the flower
with their tongue.
I wish I was a butterfly,
so I could see flowers every day,
because they are beautiful.

Elva Webb (7)
The Howbridge Infant School, Witham

What Am I?

Eight legs and they are skinny legs.
Legs look like sticks when they stand still and walk.
Some are small, some are big.
Has tusks under its body.
Tickles when it's on my hand.

A spider.

Rio King (7)
The Howbridge Infant School, Witham

Snail

Snails have a stripe of slimy goo from when they move around
Snails' habitat is the woodlands
Snails have antennae to sense enemies
The pattern on their shells brings me joy
You will find me under wood in the wood
I like snails.

Sophie Jarvis (7)
The Howbridge Infant School, Witham

The Ladybirds

Ladybird, ladybird, fly away home,
There are evil bugs coming to get you,
So fly away home before you get eaten by them.
There are lots coming to get you,
So fly away home,
So you are safe from evil bugs.

Jack Nice (6)
The Howbridge Infant School, Witham

What Am I?

Can help plants grow,
Have no eyes,
Live underground,
Like the dirt,
Have no legs,
Wiggle about to move.

Christopher Weeks (7)
The Howbridge Infant School, Witham

What Am I?

Can leave a slimy trail.
Live in trees when it's winter.
Glow when they need to find a new shell.
Can carry its home wherever it goes.

A snail.

Jacob Scott (6)
The Howbridge Infant School, Witham

Butterfly

Butterflies are beautiful,
Butterflies are colourful,
Their wings are symmetrical,
They like to flit,
Butterflies like the flowers.

Abby Brooks (6)
The Howbridge Infant School, Witham

Caterpillar

Here is a caterpillar crawling through the door.
Now it is making a cocoon so colourful and dainty.
The cocoon looks like it will crack soon, *crack!*
Here is a butterfly in my window.
Do you like butterflies?

Grace Austin-Hunt (7)
The Howbridge Infant School, Witham

Untitled

Bees fly away,
they fly to flowers and they make honey,
they can sing to you,
they fly every day,
the sun comes out every day.

Kye Bedford-Ingram (7)
The Howbridge Infant School, Witham

Tadpoles

Tadpoles turn into frogs
And they lay eggs
And their eggs don't come off
And they have a little frog on their backs
And they hop away.

Lara Anderson (6)
The Howbridge Infant School, Witham

Snails

Snails move very slowly along.
Snails leave slime trails wherever they go.
Some snails have big shells, they carry them everywhere.
Underneath it's very slimy and gooey.

Alicia Champion (7)
The Howbridge Infant School, Witham

Young Writers Information

We hope you have enjoyed reading this book - and that you will continue to enjoy it in the coming years.

If you like reading and writing poetry drop us a line, or give us a call, and we'll send you a free information pack.

Alternatively if you would like to order further copies of this book or any of our other titles, then please give us a call or log onto our website at www.youngwriters.co.uk.

A platform for your poetry!

Young Writers Information
Remus House
Coltsfoot Drive
Peterborough
PE2 9JX
(01733) 890066

Get in touch!